OLD ENGLISH SCHOLARSHIP IN ENGLAND FROM 1566-1800

BY

ELEANOR N. ADAMS, Ph.D.

ARCHON BOOKS
1970

420
A 2110

[*Yale Studies in English, Vol. 55*]

70 _ 8316

SBN: 208 00913 2
Library of Congress Catalog Card Number: 70-91177
Printed in the United States of America

For artes are like to okes, which by little and little grow a long time, afore they come to their full bigness. . . . *If you will compare the first and the last printer together and seek whether deserveth more praise and commendation, ye shall find that the first did farre exceede the last: for the last had help of manye, and the first had help of none. So that the first lighteth the candle of knowledge (as it were) and the second does but snuff it.*

Art of Reason
RAPHE LEVER
1573

PREFACE

In the study of English literature there comes to each of us a realization that one period of our language is wholly obsolete, and if we would read the literature of that period, we must apply ourselves with diligence to the perusal of grammars, dictionaries, and carefully prepared texts. A fact that we do not so often recognize is that there was no English scholarship, in the strict sense, when Old English was a spoken language. How and when did this scholarship begin? How did it develop, and what obstacles did it meet? It is the object of this thesis to discuss the beginnings of Old English scholarship, and to trace its progress until it took a recognized place in the scholarly world. The definite limits of this consideration are the publication of the first Old English book, 1566, and the establishment of the first professorship of the language in an English university, 1795. The material is chronologically presented, both in the essay and in the appendixes. Each appendix is so arranged as to illustrate a particular phase of Old English scholarship. There are some things which I do not attempt to discuss; one is the subject of runes. That subject belongs to a linguistic study, not to an historical essay. Again, I do not attempt to estimate the scholarship of that time as compared with ours of to-day. Our debt to these early scholars is not lessened by a frank recognition of the fact that their work is practically worthless to the modern student. They are the pioneers, who blazed a trail which has now become a broad highway. Yet again, I have not tried to include all early students

5

of Old English, nor to analyze every one of their publications.

What I have endeavored to do is to select such incidents, whether in the life of a scholar or in the history of a book, as will illustrate the various stages of Old English scholarship before its general recognition as a collegiate study. The task of collecting and methodizing materials has been arduous, but it has been rendered pleasant by the hope that it might serve to connect a literary movement of a peculiar kind with the general political, religious, and literary history of England. The collection of materials would have been impossible without the constant encouragement of Mr. Falconer Madan, Bodley's Librarian, to whom my most grateful acknowledgments are due for help and suggestions, as they are also due to the late Professor Arthur S. Napier, of Oxford University, for criticisms; to Mr. Horace Hart, Comptroller of the Clarendon Press, for information about Anglo-Saxon types; and to Professor Albert S. Cook, of Yale, for specific revisions and general supervision of the work. To him, also, I am much indebted for his careful proof-reading.

For collation and revision of passages quoted in the following pages, I acknowledge indebtedness to the library staff of Yale, the Bodleian, and the Public Library of Cincinnati. I am particularly grateful to Dr. Helen Price, Professor of Latin in Oxford College, for her proof-reading of Latin excerpts throughout the work.

CONTENTS

OLD ENGLISH SCHOLARSHIP IN ENGLAND

CHAPTER I

The Beginnings of Old English Scholarship in the Sixteenth Century

The wave of classical learning which swept northward through Europe into England did much towards extinguishing national literature, by the very contempt it inspired for the vulgar tongue.[1] It is therefore not to the English Renaissance, but to the Reformation, that we must look for awakened interest in Old English literature. This interest was, in its beginnings, antiquarian and controversial.

So confusing was the unrest of the Reformation that men could not distinguish clearly between the affairs of civil and ecclesiastical life. In order to lay any foundation for their new institutions, the Reformers had to establish a precedent for their beliefs. Such precedent they sought in the liturgy and sermons of the 'primitive church', and in the laws of their Anglo-Saxon forebears. Their first concern was to justify, by historical documents, their attitude towards the sacrament, the secular privileges of the clergy, and the use of the Scriptures in the vernacular. We may assume, therefore, that Old English scholarship had its definite beginnings in the controversial efforts of Archbishop Parker, John Joscelyn, his secretary, William Lambarde, record-keeper of London Tower, and John Foxe, the martyrologist. The interest of this group of men

[1] 'Amonge all the nacions, in whome I haue wandered, for the knowledge of thynges (moste benygne soueraygne) I haue founde nene so negligent and vntoward, as I haue found England in the due serch of theyr auncyent hystoryes, to the syngulare fame and bewtye therof.'—John Bale, 'Dedicatory Epistle' to *The Laboryouse Journey of John Leland*, 1549.

11

in Old English records was definite, energetic, and historical. They gave to the world the first-fruits of Old English research. Since the underlying interest was antiquarian, even with the Reformers, and since, after the definite need of old records for controversial purposes ceased, antiquarian enthusiasm nurtured 'Saxon' learning for several generations, we may properly begin the account of Old English scholarship with the book-collectors, Leland and Bale.

John Leland (1506-1552) was a resident of both Cambridge and Oxford, at a time when learning was at a very low ebb in England. He sought knowledge on the Continent, whence he returned with a great reputation as a scholar, and became successively chaplain to Henry VIII, his library-keeper, and finally, under royal commission, 'king's antiquary,[1] to serche after England's Antiquities and to peruse the libraries of all cathedrals, abbyes, priories, colleges, &c, as also all places wherein records, writings and secrets of Antiquity were reposited.' Before the final dissolution of the monasteries,[2] he spent six years searching the kingdom for rare books and manuscripts. Of these he made vast catalogues and copious notes.[3] It was Leland's purpose to use all the materials collected during his six years' journey for compiling a history of Britain, with all its shires and families, from the earliest times to his own day; but he died before his scheme was completed.[4] Bale says of him:

I was as famylyarlye acquaynted wyth hym, as wyth whome I am best acquaynted, and do knowe certenlye, that he from his youth was so ernestly study-

---

[1] 25 Henry VIII (1533).

[2] 31 Henry VIII (1537).

[3] In recognition of his labors, Henry VIII appointed Leland canon of what is now Christ Church, Oxford.

[4] Cf. the work of Camden, Lambarde, Verstegan, Carew, etc.

ouse and desyerouse of our Antiquytees, that alwayes hys whole stodyes were dyrected to that ende. And for the true and full attaynynge therunto, he not onlye applyed hym selfe to the knowledge of the Greke and Latyne tongues, . . . but also to the stodye of the Bryttyshe, Saxonyshe, and Walshe tongues, and so muche profyted therin, that he most perfitelye vnderstode them.[1]

Leland was, as Gibson says in his *Life of Camden,* the first man to turn the eyes of the kingdom toward English antiquity.[2] Whatever may have been his ability as a scholar, there is no doubt that his *Laboryouse Journey* 'brought out of deadly darkenesse to lyuelye lyght . . . the monumentes of auncyent wryters, . . . and conserued many good authors, the whych otherwyse had ben lyke to haue peryshed, to the no small incomodyte of good letters.'[3]

Leland was a very epicure among antiquaries. Throughout his notes he shows plainly that his interest in the books he collected centred in the splendid bindings, the exquisite illuminations, the beauty of the copy-hand, and the rarity or quaintness of the subject-matter. Their polemic interest had little weight with him. With John Bale (1495-1563) the case was different; although a Carmelite monk converted to Protestantism, and very zealous for the Reformation, he bitterly regretted the destruction attending the disso-

---

[1] Bale, Preface to Leland's *Laboryouse Journey.*

[2] Lambarde, Holinshed, Camden, Dugdale, and Stowe are indebted to his collections.

[3] Cf. Leland's *Laboryouse Journey.* Edward VI ordered Leland's papers to be preserved, finally entrusting them to Sir John Cheke. After Edward's death, Cheke gave four volumes of papers (*The Itinerary*) to Humphrey Purefoy. Purefoy's son gave them to William Burton in 1612. Burton obtained eight other volumes, and in 1632 deposited them all in the Bodleian Library. A great many of the rest of Leland's manuscripts found their way into the Cottonian collection.

lution of the monasteries.[1] Twice he was exiled to
Germany and Switzerland, but died as prebend of
Canterbury in his sixty-eighth year, 'leaving', says
Fuller, 'a scholar's inventory, more books (many of his
own making) than money behind him'. Without royal
patronage, and often in exile, Bale collected books
with the instinct of the antiquary and the zeal of the
reformer. In this collecting he was encouraged and
probably employed by Matthew Parker, who after
Bale's death obtained part of his collection.[2] As a
reformer, Parker was noted for his conservatism, his
even balance, and his executive ability, rather than for
his scholarship. In his polemic use of antiquarian collections, he may have been influenced by Matthias
Flacius (Illyricus), a follower of Luther, who in May,
1561, wrote to Parker from Jena, urging him to collect
historical manuscripts for ecclesiastical purposes, and
to place in safe-keeping in large libraries such books
in private hands or remote places as might illustrate
'the obscured Truth of the Church and reprove the
Popish Tyranny'.[3] Bale, as well as Parker, came under
the influence of Flacius and his characteristic formula,
Historia est fundamentum doctrinæ.[4] It is hardly to be

[1] 'I dolorouslye lamente so greate an ouersyght in the most lawfull
ouerthrow of the . . . Abbeyes and Fryeryes, when the most worthy
monumentes of this realme, so myserably peryshed in the spoyle. Oh,
that men of learnyng and of perfyght loue to their nacyon, were not then
appoynted to the serche of theyr lybraryes, for the conseruacyon of those
most noble Antiquitees.'—Bale, 'Dedicatory Epistle' to *The Laboryouse
Journey of John Leland.*

[2] Cf. Lane Poole, *John Bale's Index*, 1902, and letter of Parker to Lord
Burleigh in *Parker Correspondence*, edited for the Parker Society.

[3] Cf. Strype, *Life of Parker*, Bk. 2, chap. 9, ed. 1711. Strype prints the
letter of Flacius in the appendix, no. XVIII; the original is in C. C. C.,
MS. CXIX, art. 47. For an account of Flacius, cf. *Allgemeine Deutsche
Biographie.*

[4] The suggestions of Flacius were amply developed by Parker, as witness his gift of books to Benet College; and his great work, the *De Antiquitate Britannicæ Ecclesiæ*, 1572. Cf. also the letters-patent issued to
Parker in 1568.

expected that the Continental scholar thought of *historia* except as found in Latin and Greek manuscripts, but fortunately the English Reformers placed emphasis on documents in the vulgar tongue, else we should have less than our remnant of Old English literature. One is led to futile conjecture as to how many Old English manuscripts were thrown into the scrap-heap when the Continent was flooded with monastic treasures after the Dissolution.[1] A fair copy of a well-known Latin or Greek author was far more acceptable than an original document in the 'Saxon' tongue, except in England, where there was already awakened the spirit of nationalism, which was soon to find a glorious expression in Elizabethan literature.

Two other industrious antiquaries, Robert Talbot (1505?-1558) and George Owen (d. 1558), contributed to the store of manuscripts used by the Reformers. Talbot was Fellow of New College, Oxford. At various times he held ecclesiastical preferments in Essex, Northampton, Norfolk, and Berkshire, which perhaps enabled him to indulge his taste for collecting old manuscripts.[2] Wood says of Talbot that he was 'very much esteemed in his time, and after, for his singular knowledge in the Antiquities of England, and for his care in preserving and collecting ancient books and monuments decayed by time'.[3] Owen, a Fellow of Merton College, Oxford, was physician to Henry VIII, to Edward VI, and to Mary. From Henry VIII he received large grants of land about Oxford, including Durham College[4] and Godstow Nunnery, where his

---

[1] Cf. Appendix IV.

[2] He prepared *Annotationes in eam partim Itinerarii Antonini quæ ad Britanniam pertinet.* This is printed in the third volume of Hearne's edition of Leland's *Itinerary*, 1710-12.

[3] Cf. Wood, *Athenæ Oxonienses*, Vol. 1, col. 263, ed. 1813.

[4] Sold to Sir Thomas Pope as the site for Trinity College.

family lived for some time.[1] Strype says that Archbishop Parker secured many books, 'some Saxon, from Robert Talbot, a great Collector of such ancient writings in K. Henry the Eighth's time, an acquaintance of Leland and Bale'. Some of these, he adds, Talbot had from Dr. Owen, from whom also Parker obtained books.[2] Other collections belonging to Talbot were given to Benet College, Cambridge, the Archbishop obtaining them through his own interest and that of Bale, Dr. Caius, and others.

It has already been indicated that the dominant figure among sixteenth century 'Saxonists' was Matthew Parker (1504-1575). As Master of Benet College (Corpus Christi), and Vice-Chancellor of Cambridge University,[3] he had every opportunity to cultivate his taste for book-collecting and other antiquarian pursuits. During the fifteen years that he was Archbishop of Canterbury, he devoted his best efforts to defining the discipline and beliefs of the newly constituted Church of England. To him are due the Thirty-nine Articles, and the translation of the Scriptures commonly known as the 'Bishops' Bible'.[4] Through the influence of Catherine Parr, Parker was appointed one of a commission of three to examine the condition of Cambridge, which with Oxford faced a danger like that of the monastic dissolution. The report of this

[1] Wood says that Owen witnessed Henry VIII's will. He laments that the learned writings of this man are lost, 'so consequently posterity is depriv'd of some matters in them which might be grateful to curious readers'.—*Athenæ Oxonienses*, Vol. 1, col. 275.

[2] Cf. Cotton Vitellius D. 7: A Collection of Charters written out by Joscelyn; to some he adds notes as: 'The copy of this Dr. Talbot had of Dr. Owen'; 'the Archbishop of Canterbury had this Charter from Dr. Owen'.—Strype, *Life of Parker* 4. 529.

[3] Master of Benet, 1544-53; Vice-Chancellor, 1544-5, 1548-9; Archbishop of Canterbury, 1559-1574.

[4] 1568-72.

committee did much to avert collegiate dissolution. The Archbishop was very liberal in his gifts of books to Cambridge. To Benet College alone he gave one hundred volumes, among which were many Old English manuscripts, including the Gospels, Alfred's translation of Gregory's *Pastoral Care*, and the *Anglo-Saxon Chronicle*.[1] Andrew Perne, Vice-Chancellor at the time of these gifts, added materially to the collection while visiting Parker at Lambeth.

Parker is noteworthy as a patron of Old English learning, but as an author he is not entitled to very high rank, since he was greatly aided in all of his learned works by his secretary, John Joscelyn. As an editor he was very industrious, but has been repeatedly accused of taking great liberties in altering the texts of his originals.[2] In his scriptorium at Lambeth, the illuminators, transcribers, engravers, and bookbinders were

[1] Cf. M. R. James, *The Sources of Archbishop Parker's Collections of MSS.*, 1899, for a full list of these books.

[2] 'He kept such in his Family, as could imitate any of the old Characters admirably well. One of these was Lyly, . . . that could counterfeit any antique Writing. Him the Archbishop customarily used to make old Books Compleat, that wanted some Pages; that the Character might seem to be the same throughout.'—Strype, *Life of Parker* 4. 529.

Parker, in a letter to Cecil dated Jan. 24, 1565-6, says:

'I return you your book again, and thank you for the sight thereof. I account it much worth the keeping, as well for the fair antique writing with the Saxon interpretation, as also for the strangeness of the translation, which is neither the accustomed old text, neither St. Jerome's, nor yet the Septuaginta. I had thought to have made up the want of the beginning of the Psalter, for it wanteth the first psalm, and three verses in the second psalm, and methought the leaf going before the xxvith psalm would have been a meet beginning before the whole Psalter, having David sitting with his harp or psaltery decachordo vel ogdochordo, with his ministers with their tubis ductilibus et cymbalis sonoris, &c, and then the first psalm written on the back side; which I was in mind to have caused Lyly to have counterfeited in antiquity, &c., but that I called to remembrance that ye have a singular artificer to adorn the same, which your honour shall do well to have the monument finished, or else I shall cause it to be done and remitted again to your library.'—*Parker Correspondence*, CXCIV.

kept busy, while from the press of John Day, in his little shop over Aldersgate, there issued in the eight years between 1566 and 1574 the first books printed in Anglo-Saxon type, which Parker had procured for this purpose.

And for Learning, his House was a kind of flourishing University of Learned Men: And his Domesticks, being provoked by the Archbishop's Exhortations and Precepts, often published to the World the fruits of their Studies. . . . He would admit none to live under him, but such as truly and sincerely feared God, and beside their daily Attendance, employed themselves at their leisure Hours, in some kind of laudable exercise: as in Reading, making Collections, transcribing, Composing, Painting, Drawing or some other Application of Learning or Art.[1] . . . As the Archbishop had the chief Care of the Church and of Religion under the Queen, so had he also of the venerable Antiquity of the Nation, whose great skill therein, and earnest desire of retrieving the ancient Stories and Accounts of Persons and Things, in these Islands, from the Times of the Britains and Saxons, was so well known, that a kind of Office was granted him, for the Preservation of these Antiquities, and the Privy Council granted him their Countenance, to gather up ancient Monuments throughout England, in whose Possession soever they were; not indeed to keep or convert to his own Use, but to have the Sight and Reading of them.[2]

In July, 1568, a letter was issued authorizing the Archbishop to have

special Care and Oversight, in the Conservation of such ancient Records and Monuments as were written of the State and Affairs of the Realm of England and Ireland; which were heretofore preserved and recorded, by special Appointment of Certain of her Majesties Ancestors, in divers Abbies, to be Treasurehouses to keep and leave in Memory such Occurences, as fell in

[1] Cf. Strype, *Life of Parker* 4. 502.

[2] Strype, *Life of Parker* 3. 19. 263.

their Times. And because divers of such Writings were commen into the Hands of private Persons, and so partly remained Obscure and Unknown; They willed and required, that when the same Archbishop should send his Letters, or learned Deputies, requesting a sight of any such ancient Records, that they would . . . gently impart the same: Not meaning to withdraw them from the Owners, but for a time to peruse the same, upon Promise, or Band given of making Restitution.[1]

This letter gave Parker's agents unbounded authority for procuring rare books, and was especially valuable in case the owners refused to deliver their treasures. Whatever 'restitution' may have been offered, it is to be doubted if many books were ever returned to their owners. So zealously did Parker exercise his prerogative, that one agent alone professed to have gathered six thousand seven hundred books within four years.[2]

The bishops were asked to report the books in their cathedral churches and dioceses, especially if any 'Saxon' books were found. An extract from a letter written to Parker by Bishop Jewel of Salisbury indicates how very meagre was the knowledge of Old English manuscripts among the learned men of the sixteenth century.

---

[1] This letter was signed by Nic. Bacon, Th. Norfolk, W. Northampton, R. Leicester, W. Howard, W. Cecyl, members of the Privy-Council, July 7, 1568.

[2] 'Thys reuerende Father by vertue of Commission from oure soueraigne Queene hyr maiestic, didde cause to be diligently gathered many bookes of antiquitie. . . . Wythin four yeares, of Diuinitie, Astronomie, Historie, Phisicke, and others of sundrye Artes and Sciences (as I can truly auouche, hauing his Grace's Commission whereunto his hande is yet to be seene) *six thousand seauen hundred* Bookes, by my onelye trauaile; wherof choyse becing taken, he moste gratiouslye bestowed many on Corpus Christi Colledge in Cambridge. I was not the onelye man in this businesse.' —Stephen Batman, *Doome Warning all men to Judgemente,* 1581, pp. 399-400.

. . . It may please your Grace to understand, that according to my Promise, I have ransacked our poor library of Salisbury, and have found nothing worthy the finding, saving only one Book written in the *Saxon* Tongue; which I mind to send your Grace by the next Convenient Messenger.[1] The Book is of reasonable Bigness, well near as thick as the Communion Book. Your Grace hath three or four of the same Size. It may be *Alfricus* for all my Cunning. But your Grace will soon find what he is. Other certain Books there are of *Rabanus* and *Anselmus*, but as common so also little worth. If I had any Leisure I would send your Grace the titles of all. But as now I am entering into the Visitation of my Dioces. By the way, if I may hear of any Antiquities, I will do your Grace to understand. Thus I humbly take my leave from Sarum, the 18ᵗʰ of January 1568.

Your Graces most humble

Jo. Sarum.[2]

John Joscelyn, Parker's secretary and co-worker, gives the following quaint and enthusiastic account of the Archbishop:

He thought he could not bestow his laboure better on anye thinge (considerynge the place which he occupied) then in the busie searche off the opinion off the Doctores of his tyme and conferringe them with the writers off all ages. Besides he was verie carefull and not without some charges to knowe the religion off thancient fatheres and those especially which were off the Englishe Churche. Therfore in seekinge upp the Chronicles off the Brittones and Englishe Saxons which laye hidden euery wheare contemned and buried in forgetfullness and through the ignorance of the Languages not wel vnderstanded his owen especially and his mens dilegince wanted not. And to the ende that

---

[1] The book was sent to Parker on Jan. 31.

[2] This letter Strype says he found in a folio volume in the Public Library of Cambridge, 'the book being S. Gregory's Tract, *De Cura Pastorali* turned Paraphrastically into Saxon'. The same letter in a more archaic spelling is in Wanley's catalogue (Hickes' *Thesaurus*), p. 153.

these antiquities might last longe and be carefullye kept he caused them beenge broughte into one place to be well bounde and trymly covered. And yet not so contented he indeuored to sett out in printe certaine off those aunciente monuments whearoff he knew very fewe examples to be extante and which he thoughte woulde be most profitable for the posterytye to instruct them in the faythe and religion of the elders.[1]

Such were the collections and the methods used by sixteenth-century 'Saxonists'. Not only were their efforts crude, but their scheme was based on a misunderstanding of the Old English language, which they sought to interpret on the basis of Latin Grammar.[2] There is no reliable evidence of an attempt to study Old English before the middle of the sixteenth century; yet the early 'Saxonists' believed a tradition to the effect that the monks of Tavistock Abbey in Devonshire taught 'Saxon' before the Reformation. Parker himself says that the language was taught in certain abbeys, in order to preserve to the monks the knowledge of their early charters. Tavistock, he declares, had such a school, and a collection of Old English books.[2] Unfortunately we do not know what authority Parker may have had for such a statement,[3] but the tradition

---

[1] Cf. *Historiola: A litel storye of the Actes and life of Matthew now Archbischoppe of Canterb.* Imprinted 1574. Also *Historiola Collegii Corporis Christi, John Josselin,* edited for the Cambridge Antiquarian Society by John Willis Clark, 1880.

[2] This fundamental error prevented any real development in Old English scholarship until the nineteenth century. For a discussion of the Latin fallacy in Old English grammar, cf. chap. III, pp. 85-92.

[3] 'Quem in finem superioribus sæculis a maioribus nostris monialium quædam collegia instituta sunt, in quibus essent qui & huius linguæ scientia imbuerentur & eandem (cum aliis communicando) ad posteros transmitterent. Quod quidem in cœnobio monialium Tauestockensi in comitatu Deuoniæ & multis aliis conuenticulis (nostra memoria) receptum fuit, credo, ne ejus sermonis peritia, ob linguæ insolentiam penitus obsolesceret.'—Matthew Parker, preface to his edition of Asser's *Ælfredi Regis Res Gestæ,* 1574.

grew in popularity until in the seventeenth and eighteenth centuries it was assumed not only that 'Saxon'
was taught in Tavistock, but also that an Old English
grammar was printed there before the Reformation.[1]
The well known skill of the monks in the art of book-
making renders it possible that they may have copied
Old English manuscripts, even if they did not know
the language; but that any 'Saxon' printing was done

[1] 'But what this convent was chiefly celebrated for was the laudable
Institution of a Saxon School erected for the teaching of the Saxon Language, that the Antiquities, Laws and Histories written in that tongue by
our Ancestors might be preserved from oblivion: and the early Patronage
of the Art of Printing, soon after the Invention thereof, met with here as
appears by several Antient Books printed in this Monastery. . . . The
Saxon School is now employed to hold Corn, Hay, &c.'—Brown Willis,
History of Mitred Parliamentary Abbeys, 1718, 1. 171.

Camden, in his *Remains*, told the story of the Tavistock school, while
Bishop Gibson, in his edition of Camden, 1722, adds: 'This School, in which
the Saxon Tongue was taught, is still in being; and (as I have heard) there
was also at the beginning of the late Civil war, a Saxon Grammar printed
in Tavistocke', 1. 31. A little later, Gough, in editing Camden (1789),
says: 'The foundation here for the encouragement of Saxon literature
probably sunk at the Reformation'. Then he adds: 'The anecdote of a
Saxon Grammer being printed here in the beginning of the late Civil War
(a very unlikely period) rests on the single Authority of bishop Gibson, or
Dʳ. Musgrave, who sent him many particulars relating to this county',
1. 33. Hearne, in the Appendix to Heming's *Chartulary*, p. 662, says: 'Mr.
Bagford would have stuck at no price for a grammar printed at Tavistock,
commonly called *The Long Grammar*'. James Ingram seems to have accepted the Tavistock tradition as late as 1807; cf. his *Inaugural Lecture on
the Utility of Anglo-Saxon Literature*.

Petheram, in his *Historical Sketch of the Progress and Present State of
Anglo-Saxon Literature*, 1840, ascribes the probable origin of the Tavistock-
grammar story to a misapprehension regarding a copy of Boethius, printed
in English at Tavistock by Dan Thomas Rychard, 1525. Of this *Boke of
Comfort*, Hearne, in his gloss to Robert of Gloucester, says that the translation was made by Walton, canon of Oseney, and printed 'out of a pious
design as well as for the advancing of the Saxon Tongue, which was taught
in this Abbey, as in some other places of this kingdom, with success: and
there were lectures read in it here (Tavistock), which continued some time
after the Reformation. . . . From having a variety of words agreeing
with the Saxon, it (Boethius) might be thought a very proper book for the
attaining to a knowledge of the Saxon language.'

is highly improbable, since Parker himself, in the same book in which he mentions the Tavistock school, declares that the 'Saxon' types he procured for Day the printer in 1566 were the first ever cut.[1] There remains to-day no substantial evidence of Old English learning, manuscripts, or grammar at Tavistock.[2] Whatever feeble knowledge of the language may have existed in the monasteries inevitably perished at the Dissolution.

The first Old English ever printed is to be found in *A Testimonie of Antiquitie.*[3] The book is undated, but was issued, presumably, in 1566-67.[4] For the reproduction of the Old English text, Parker furnished his printer, John Day, with a font of Anglo-Saxon types.[5] The volume contains:

(a) Preface to the Christian Reader [English, with Old English quotations].

(b) A Sermon of the Paschall Lambe and of the sacramentall body and bloud of Christ our Sauiour,

[1] Cf. Appendix III.

[2] 'No traces however of such a book [Tauistock grammar] can now be found, and it may have been a mere error arising from the inadequate manner in which some people formerly applied the term Anglo-Saxon'.— Wright, *Essay on the Literature of the Anglo-Saxons*, p. 109.

[3] 'A Testimonie of Antiqvitie, shewing the Auncient fayth in the Church of England touching the Sacrament of the body and bloude of the Lord here publikely preached, and also receaued in the Saxons tyme, aboue 600 years agoe. Jeremie. 6. Goe into the Streets, and inquyre for the olde way: and it be the good and ryght way, then goe therin, that ye maye finde rest for your soules. But they say: we will not walke therein. Imprinted at London by John Day, dwelling ouer Aldersgate beneath S. Martyns.'

[4] The *London Book Trade Directory* has a list of Day's publications for sale between 17 Nov.–Dec. 31. 9 Eliz. (1566), among which is entered *A Testimonie of Antiquity.* This would indicate that the book was printed as early as 1566. Cf. Arber, *Transcript of Registers of the Company of Stationers of London*, Vol. 5, 1554-1640.

[5] 'Iam vero cum Dayus Typographus primus (& omnium certe quod sciam solus) has formas æri inciderit facile quæ Saxonicis literis perscripta sunt, iisdem typis diuulgabuntur.'—Parker, Preface to Asser's *Ælfredi Regis Res Gestæ*, 1574.

written in the olde Saxon tounge before the Conquest
and appoynted in the reigne of the Saxons to be vnto
the people at Easter before they shoulde receaue the
Communion and now first translated into our common
English Speche[1] [Old English, with parallel English
translation].

(c) Epistle of Alfrike abbot of S. Albons and of
Malmesberye to Wulfsine byshop of Scyrburne[2] [Old
English, with parallel English translation].

(d) Epistle to Wulfstane[3] [Latin].

(e) The Lordes prayer, the Creede and the X Com-
maundements in the Saxon and English Tounge.

The preface is largely discursive on doctrines of the
Church; it is probably the work of John Joscelyn,
rather than of Parker. A few extracts will show the
controversial nature of this curious old book:[4]

Great contention hath nowe been of longe tyme
about the moste comfortable sacrament of the body
and bloud of Christ our Sauiour. . . . But that
thou mayest knowe (good Christian reader) how this
is aduouched more boldly than truely, . . . here is
set forth vnto thee a testimonye of verye auncient
tyme, wherin is plainly shewed what was the iudge-
ment of the learned men in thys matter, in the dayes

[1] 'This sermon is found in diuerse bookes of sermon, written in the olde
Englishe or Saxon tongue: whereof two bookes bee nowe in the handes of
the most reuerend father the Archbishop of Caunterburye.'—Notes in
A Testimonie.

[2] 'Here followeth the wordes of Elfrike—It is founde in a booke of the
olde Saxon tounge wherin be XLII chapters of canons . . . and this
epistle is also in a canon booke of the Churche of Exeter.'—*Ibid.*

[3] Wulfstan's Epistle is rendered from 'fayre bokes written of olde in
the Cathedrall Churches of Worcester and Excester'. It is given in Latin,
for 'verye fewe there be that doe understande the old Englishe or Saxon.'
—*Ibid.*

[4] The Archbishop 'sought much after Saxon Antiquities, and many of
them he made subservient to the Vindication of our Reformation in oppo-
sition to Popery: and particularly Saxon Translations of the Scripture.'
—Strype, *Life of Parker* 4. 535.

of the Saxons before the conquest. Fyrst thou hast here a Sermon or homelye, for the holy day of Easter, written in the olde Englishe or Saxon speech, which doth of set purpose and at large, intreate of thys doctryne, and is found among many other Sermons in the same olde speech, made for other festiuall dayes and sondayes of the yeare, and vsed to be spoken orderly accordyng to those daies vnto the people, as by the bokes themselues it doth well appear. And of such Sermons be yet manye bookes to be seene, partlye remayning in priuate mens handes, and taken out from monasteryes at their dissolution: partlye yet reserued in the libraryes of Cathedrall Churches, as of Worcester, Hereford and Exeter. From which places diuerse of these bookes haue bene deliuered into the handes of the most reuerend father, Matthewe Archbyshop of Caunterburye, by whose diligent search for such writings of historye, and other monumentes of antiquitie, as might reueale vnto vs what hath ben the state of our church in England from tyme to tyme, these thynges that bee here made knowen vnto thee, do come to lyght. . . . We let passe many good gospells, which he that lyste may translate. For we dare not enlarge thys boke much further, lest it be ouer great & so cause to men lothsomnes through his bygnes.[1]

Rowe Mores[2] asserts that there were two editions of *A Testimonie* within a year, but there is not sufficient difference in the existing copies to prove this statement. However, large excerpts from the Old English, and translations of them, continue to appear almost to the end of the eighteenth century.[3]

Among the curiosities of Old English printing is

[1] The book is small octavo. To all contained in the volume the signature of Parker and fourteen bishops is set, attesting its endorsement.

[2] Cf. Edward Rowe Mores, *Typographical Founders*, 1778.

[3] Extracts in Foxe's *Actes and Monuments*, 1570, etc.; English translations, Oxford, 1675; London, 1685, 1736. For new edition by L'Isle, 1623, cf. chap. II, pp. 45 ff.

A Defence of Priests' Marriages.[1] The character of the book is thus outlined by Strype:

> In the time of his Recess under Q. Mary, he [Parker] writ in English (or rather enlarged with his own Additions) a Learned Book of the Mariage of Priests, showing the Lawfulness thereof. . . . Which he caused to be printed (concealing his Name) soon after the Synod, anno 1562. . . . This book came forth with the Archbishop's Preface. . . . For the Excellency of the Matters contained in those Additions, the Book is most valuable. They give an Historical Account of the Mariage of Priests from before the Conquest, in the Saxon Times, and bring it down to the Reign of K. Edward VI, out of the Ancient Writers of our own Nation and the Saxon Chronologies; and some of the Allegations are set down in the Saxon Tongue.[2]

Presumably a tract by John Ponet,[3] bishop of Winchester, forms the basis of Parker's *Defence.* In a few copies only, and these intended for gift-books,[4] Parker inserted the specimens of Old English to which Strype refers. Strype explains the use of the Old English in so few copies on the ground that the language was obsolete, and hence unintelligible to many readers. Such extracts, he thinks, would hinder rather than help the circulation of the book. This opinion is ingenious on the part of the Archbishop's biographer, but we may be sure that it would take more than four meagre quotations in a strange tongue to kill a controversial tract in the thick of Reformation debates. It is more reasonable to assume that the few copies

[1] In 1561 Queen Elizabeth expressed her displeasure at the marriage of the clergy, and prohibited women from living in college and cathedral precincts.

[2] Cf. Strype, *Life of Parker* 4. 504-5.

[3] Ponet wrote two tracts on the subject of priests' marriages: the first printed in London, by Reginald Wolff, 1549; the second (on which Parker based his *Defence*) printed on the continent, 1555-56.

[4] John Parker, son of the Archbishop, is authority for this statement.

are indicative of Parker's pride in his new Anglo-Saxon types,[1] and that these copies are, as it were, an *édition de luxe*. Both the original and the enlarged editions are undated, but Strype's mention of 1562 has furnished a conjectural date,[2] pointing to an earlier use of Anglo-Saxon type than that in *A Testimonie of Antiquitie*. The *Stationers' Registers* show that *A Defence* was licensed in 1566-67, and not advertised for sale in the *Book Trade Directory* before 1567. It is at once evident that Parker, who employed Jugge to print the enlarged copies of *A Defence*, used his new Anglo-Saxon types (procured for John Day) shortly after he published *A Testimonie*.[3] This book furnishes the only evidence that another printer used these types during Day's lifetime. Moreover, we may consider it as the first semi-historical essay based on Old English sources.

William Lambarde (1536-1601) was, next to Parker, the most important worker in the sixteenth-century revival of Old English. He was a member of Lincoln's Inn, living for a time in chambers with Laurence Nowell, through whom he first became interested in the study of Old English. Nowell made some collec-

---

[1] The specimens of Old English, from the *Anglo-Saxon Chronicle* and from church 'offices', are on pp. 288, 306, 308, 346 of *A Defence*, printed by Jugge. The original edition (without the specimens) was printed by J. Kinston for R. Jugge. There are some differences in pagination in the two issues, as well as differences in type and spelling in the added portions, clearly indicating resetting of some leaves. For a full discussion of the two issues, see *Athenæum*, Dec. 31, 1910.

[2] Bodleian Catalogue, British Museum Catalogue, and Bohn's *Catalogue of Rare Books*, have a tentative date (1562?).

[3] *Stationers' Registers*, 22 July 1566–22 July, 9 Eliz. (1567), has the following entry: 'Recevyed of Master Jugge for his lycense for the prynting of [a] boke entitled a defence of preestes maryages stablished by the imperiall lawes of this Realme of Englonde, . . . xijd'. The *London Book Trade Directory* enters *A Defence* under Jugge's list between 17 Nov.–31 Dec., 10 Eliz. (1567). *A Testimonie* is entered under Day's list 17 Nov.–31 Dec., 9 Eliz. (1566).

tions of Anglo-Saxon laws, and on going abroad left them for Lambarde to translate into Latin.[1] This collection, with the translation, Lambarde published in 1568 under the title of *Archaionomia*.[2] In this undertaking he was encouraged by Parker. The volume, printed by Day in Anglo-Saxon type, contains the laws of Ine, Alfred, Edward, Æthelstan, Edmund, Edgar, Æthelred, and Canute, in Old English, with parallel Latin translation. To these are added the Latin laws of William and of Edward the Confessor.[3] Some Latin explanations of Old English law-terms and titles, and an index, together with a map of England, complete the volume. The *Rerum & verborum in hoc translatione præcipue difficilium explicatio* may be considered as the first printed nucleus of an Old English vocabulary.

Less than a century later, Somner, in reading Lambarde's *Archaionomia*, found that in the 'Latin version there was a polite and elaborate stile too much

[1] Cf. preface to *Archaionomia*.

[2] 'Archaionomia, sive de priscis anglorum legibus libri, sermone Anglico, vetustate antiquissimo; aliquot abhinc seculis conscripti, atque nunc demum, magno iurisperitorum, & amantium antiquitatis omnium commodo, e tenebris in lucem vocati. Gulielmo Lambardo interprete. Regum qui has Leges scripserunt, nomenclationem, & quid præterea accesserit, altera monstrabit pagina. Londini, ex officina Joannis Daij: An. 1568. Cum gratia et privilegio Regiæ Maiestatis per Decennium.'

[3] 'In hoc opere continentur,

Leges { Inæ, Occiduorum Saxonum Regis.
{ Aluredi, totius Angliæ Regis.

Fœdus   Aluredi, & Guthruni Regum.
Leges   Edouardi, Regis Angliæ.
Fœdus   Edouardi, & Guthruni Regum.

Leges {
Ethelstani, Regis Angliæ.
Edmundi, Regis Angliæ.
Edgari,   Regis Angliæ.
Ethelredi, Regis Angliæ.
Canuti,   Regis Angliæ, Daciæ, & Noruegiæ.

Atque hac quidem omnia Latine reddidimus. Accessere præterea latine conscriptæ leges, quas Regem Edouardum (confessorem vocant) tulisse, & Gulielmum eius nominis primum approbasse. scriptores plerique omnes prædicant.'

affected, that gave little or no help to the Reader in Understanding the original Saxon'. Junius endorsed this opinion, and said he preferred the ancient version of John Brompton;[1] advising 'all that love the genuine Monuments of antiquity, rather to embrase the old interpretation of a rough and impolite age, than rashly adhere to the modern and more refined translations.'

That the laws published by Lambarde were but a fragment of the then existing manuscripts is commented on by Dr. George Hickes, who declares that, aside from other manuscripts, probably in the C. C. C. C. and Cotton libraries, he himself had laws of Æthelbert, Hlothære, and Ædric from the *Textus Roffensis*, which were not seen by Lambarde. Faulty and fragmentary as it was, Lambarde's *Archaionomia* was the only collection of Old English laws printed for a century.[2]

Lambarde's greatest work was *A Perambulation of Kent*,[3] 1576. The materials were gathered by 1570,

[1] John Brompton, Abbot of Jorvaux (1436?), to whom is ascribed the authorship of a chronicle from the coming of Augustine to the death of Richard I. The manuscript of this Latin translation of the Old English Chronicle is in C. C. C. C., and was printed in Twysden's *Historiæ Anglicanæ* (1652), col. 725-1284.

[2] This collection was highly valued as a law text-book, even by those who were unfamiliar with Old English, as witness a copy in the Bodleian, with copious notes on the Latin version in the handwriting of John Marshall, 1583, and Humphrey Davenport, 1631. In 1640 Abraham Wheloc republished *Archaionomia*, with some additions. A copy of this edition in the Bodleian has manuscript annotations by Junius, while the Old English text has been scored, corrected, and part of it retranslated. Another copy in the Bodleian has corrections and notes on the Old English in the handwriting of Dr. George Hickes.

[3] 'A Perambulation of Kent, Containing the description Hystorie and Customs of that Shyre. Collected and written (for the most part) in the year 1570 by William Lambarde of Lincolnes Inn, Gent., and now increased by the addition of some things which the Authore him selfe hath obserued since that time. Imprinted at London for Ralphe Newberie dwelling in Fleete-streete a little aboue the Conduit Anno 1576.'

when the book was sent to Thomas Wotton and to Parker for comment. It is quite probable that Lambarde knew of some laws not included in the 1568 volume, where he confined himself to translating and editing what Nowell had collected. In this shire-history, Lambarde made extensive use of Old English documents, quoting rather freely from the *Textus Roffensis*,[1] which he had found in the library of Rochester Cathedral. This book has the distinction of being the first known county-history of England, as well as the first in which we find any use of Anglo-Saxon types other than those of John Day.[2] Lambarde's power of digesting his knowledge of Anglo-Saxon law is illustrated in *Eirenarcha*, or the *Offices of the Justices of the Peace*, which ran through six editions between 1581 and 1599.[3] The publication of works on Old English law so soon after *A Testimonie of Antiquitie* is evidence of the fact that parallel to the controversial uses of the language ran a broader stream of patriotic and antiquarian interest in the nation's archives. Lambarde, as record-keeper of the Tower of London, had unusual opportunities for gathering materials.[4] That royal favor, as well as encouragement from the clergy, attended such efforts to emphasize the antiquity of English law, is illustrated in the well-known

[1] From the *Textus Roffensis* he quotes (a) a statute concerning the Rochester bridge, pp. 307-311; (b) the Mepham will, of which he says: 'That you may know as well what aduancement to Gentrie was then in use, as also what weapons iewels and ornaments were at that time worne and occupied, I wyll set before your eye, the last will and testament of one Byrhtric and his wife'; (c) a postscript to the Ang'o-Saxon laws, 'placed in diuers olde copies of the Saxon lawes, after the end of all, as a note of aduertisement'. These extracts have interlinear English translation.

[2] For Anglo-Saxon types, cf. Appendix III.

[3] In *Eirenarcha* are only a few Old English words, mostly law-terms.

[4] He projected a history similar to Camden's *Britannia;* this was not published till 1730, when it appeared as *Dictionarium Angliæ Topographicum et Historicum.*

anecdote of an interview between Queen Elizabeth and Lambarde on the occasion of his presenting her with his *Pandecta of the Tower Records*, on August 4, 1601.[1]

John Foxe (1516-1587) lived for some time in the house of John Day, working on his *Actes and Monuments*, or *Book of Martyrs*, which Day printed in 1563. In this way Foxe came under the influence of the early 'Saxonists', and in the second edition (1570) he included in his *Book of Martyrs* a large portion of *A Testimonie of Antiquitie*,[2] excluding any passages that might be construed as favorable to Roman Catholicism.[3] In 1571 he published the Gospels[4] in Old English, with a preface, and an English translation of the text. This preface Foxe wrote himself, but the editing of the text and the translation was the work of Parker[5] or Joscelyn, for there is no evidence that Foxe had any knowledge of Old English. Some extracts from the preface, addressed to Queen Elizabeth, indicate how this book was intended to prepare the way for the famous 'Bishops' Bible', 1572:[6]

[1] Cf. Strickland's *Life of Queen Elizabeth.*

[2] The two epistles of Ælfric, and the sermon against transubstantiation; cf. 2. 302-3, 304-8; these are preceded by an Old English alphabet, and followed by an English translation. The same extracts occur in the eight editions, 1570-1680.

[3] Such as legendary miracles relating to the sacrament.

[4] 'The Gospels of the fower Euangelistes translated in the olde Saxons tyme out of Latin into the vulgare toung of the Saxons, newly collected out of Auncient Monumentes of the sayd Saxons, and now published for testimonie of the Same. At London, Printed by John Daye dwelling ouer Aldersgate 1571.' These gospels were re-edited by Marshall and Junius. Dort, 1665. Cf. chap. 2, pp. 72 ff.

[5] 'We are beholden to the reuerend and learned father in God, Matthew Archbishop of Cant. a cheefe and a famous trauailler in thys the Church of England, by whose industrious diligence & learned labours this booke, with others moe, hath bene collected & serched out of the Saxons monumetes.'—Preface to the Gospels.

[6] *A Testimonie of Antiquitie* sought to prove the authenticity of the church-offices, such as the sacrament; the edition of the Gospels sought to establish the use of Scripture in the vulgar tongue.

Among other great and manifold fruites which dayly ensue by the Studyes of good men, to the publike vtilitie of the common wealth, there is none in my opinion, either at all tymes more behouefull, or at thys tyme more needefull, then the opening to this our age the tymes of old antiquities. The deficte whereof, what inconuenience it hath bredde to the Church of Christ, easie it is to see & more lamentable to consider. . . . Not to vnderstand what was done before we were borne is to liue always as children. . . . What a controuersie hath risen of late in our dayes, whether it were conuenient the Scriptures of God to be put in our Englishe tounge, wherein some more confidently then skilfully . . . haue thought it to be more dangerous to haue them in our popular language translated, considering partly the difficultie of the Scriptures in themselues, and partly the weakenesse of our vnderstanding in vs. . . . Some againe haue iudged our native Tongue unmeete to expresse God's high secret mysteries, being so barbarous & imperfecte a language as they say it is. . . . Albeit in some cases the same may serue to no small good steede, namely in courtes, and for them that be learned in the lawes, wherby they may more readily vnderstand of their olde wordes & termes, also very many deedes and Charters of Princes giftes, and foundations geuen to the church, and to Byshops Seas, and other ecclesiasticall foundations, wherein are to be seene and proued the old auncient boundes, and limites of townes, of commons, of woods, of riuers, of fieldes, & other such matters belonging to the same.[1] Howbeit not so much therfore we haue published thys treatise; but especially *to this end*, that the said boke imprinted thus in the Saxons letters may remaine in the Church as a profitable example & president of olde antiquitie, . . . so likewise haue we to vnderstond & conceaue, by the edition hereof, how the religion presently taught &

---

[1] It is evident that, while Parker had Foxe prepare the preface for theological purposes, he likewise was mindful of Lambarde's recent volume on Old English laws, although it is not directly referred to. The above extracts give some idea of the sixteenth-century conception of the value of Old English records, secular and religious.

professed in the Church at thys present, is no new reformation of thinges lately begonne, which were not before, but rather a reduction of the Church to the Pristine State of olde conformitie . . . wherof part hath bene sufficiently detected already by the godly diligence of the sayd Archbishop . . . in his boke of the *Saxon* Sermon & other treatises: part likewise remaine to be shewed, & set forth Shortly by the Lordes almightie grace, if it shall be his godnes to adde a few yeares moe to this golden peace. . . .

The year 1572 is notable in Reformation-literature for the publication of the 'Bishops' Bible' and the *De Antiquitate Britannicæ Ecclesiæ*. Ten years before, Flacius had spurred Parker on in his collecting of ecclesiastical records,[1] and this monumental work is the probable result of such collecting. The direct use of Old English is limited to a few quotations,[2] but the very nature of the book suggests how valuable were Old English documents in the undertaking. Parker's next venture as an editor was almost wholly antiquarian. In 1574 he published Asser's *Ælfredi Regis Res Gestæ*. This book is both a literary and a typographical rarity. Strype's rambling account[3] has done much to prejudice modern scholars against Parker as an editor. It would be unfair, in tracing the progress of Old English scholarship, to criticise too severely the methods of any one period. Yet Parker's methods in editing Asser illustrate the crudity of sixteenth-century scholarship. From Parker's Latin preface to Asser, and from Strype, we learn that Parker professed to have been most exact in printing his manuscript, in proof of which he was to deposit the original in Corpus Christi, Cambridge, for any one who willed to exam-

[1] Cf. p. 11.

[2] Cf. *De Antiquitate Britannicæ Ecclesiæ*, pp. 63, 103, a few lines each, in the accounts of Dunstan and of Anselm.

[3] Cf. Strype, *Life of Parker* 4. 39.

3

ine.[1]   Unfortunately, the manuscript no longer exists,[2]
but from copies of it annotated by Parker, and from
the Wise edition, made while the original was accessible,
it has been discovered that Parker interpolated many
passages from the *Annals of St. Neot,* and that he did
not hesitate to alter the spelling of his original as he
saw fit.   Stevenson points out that Parker assumed
that the *Annals of St. Neot* were also the work of Asser;
hence to him the interpolations made a fuller text of
the life.   That Parker never indicated his interpolations has brought down much criticism upon the so-
called 'forgeries'.[3]   The book was heralded as a valuable and scholarly edition, and its pretentiousness
was greatly increased by its being printed in the
Anglo-Saxon character, 'out of veneration for the
antiquity of the archetype'.   The Latin hand (Caroline
minuscule of the tenth century) was sufficiently like
that of Old English to suggest the propriety of so
printing it.   Strype suggests a possible reason which
causes us to reflect on the various channels through
which the Elizabethans were made familiar with Old
English:

> This was one of the Reasons that moved him to
> cause the Author of K. *Alfreds Life* . . . to be
> printed in those old Characters: namely, that he might
> bring on the Readers to the Study of the *Saxon* Lan-
> guage.   That being arrived to the Knowledge of the

---

[1] 'Indicio erunt ipsa prima exemplaria quæ idcirco Cantabrigiæ, in
bibliotheca collegii Corporis Christi, ad sempiternum huius rei testimonium
extare voluimus.'—Pref. to Asser.

[2] MS. Cott. Otho A XII, burned in 1731.

[3] Hook, *Lives of the Archbishops of Canterbury* 4. 505: 'A modern
editor knows that it is his business to produce a correct copy of his author's
works.   Parker thought little of editor or author, but desired, through the
writings of a man of mark, to edify the reader.   Much of what would now
be given in a note, he would have introduced by an interpolation of the
original.'   For an exhaustive criticism of Parker's edition of Asser, cf. W. H.
Stevenson, preface to *Asser's Life of King Alfred,* Oxford, 1904.

Character, they might convert their Endeavours towards the Saxon writings. From which might be reaped no small Pleasure and incredible Profit too, by the searching into ancient Monuments. Besides it was worth ones Pains to compare our Country Language, which we now use, with that obsolete and almost extinguished Speech; and while we are comparing them to observe how like they are and almost the same. And for that Cause chiefly he took care, that the four Gospels should be printed in that Language, and in the same Form of Character. And that the Reader might the more easily attain the Knowledge and understanding thereof, the English was joined with the Saxon in the Margin.[1]

In the preface to his edition of Asser, Parker commends Lambarde's book on the early laws as very helpful to those desiring to study Old English, especially the explanations of names of places and people.[2] He also observes that the Old English character is like the Irish, and that the study of the former would aid in understanding the latter, in which many ancient writings exist. The volume consists of:[3]

[1] Strype renders the above from the following portion of Parker's preface to Asser: 'Primum enim ubi huius te libelli lectioni paululum assuefeceris, literarumque priscarum gnarus iam extiteris, licebit a Latinis ad Saxonica studium conuertere, quorum ex scriptis (mihi crede) non mediocrem voluptatem adipisceres: & in veteribus monumentis perscrutandis incredibilem cum voluptate vtilitatem coniunges. Præterea operæ pretium erit patrium hunc nostrum (quo hodie vtimur) sermonem, cum illo obsoleto iam pene & extincto conferre & conferendo quam sint inter se similes, & pene eædem, animaduertere. Quam potissimum ob causam, quatuor Euangelia eadem lingua atque ijsdem, literarum formulis excudi curavimus & quo facilius eius cognitionem, intelligentiamque comprehenderes, Anglica cum Saxonicis in margine coniunximus.'

[2] 'Quibus de rebus si qua forte quis degustare concupiuerit. Gulielmi Lambardi (viri sane eruditi & in hospitio Lincolniensi inter legum consultos domestici iuris peritissimi) præfationem perlegat & expendat, quam libro de veteribus Saxonum legibus præfixit quas nuper latinis literis eleganter expressit.'

[3] With the Asser is bound Thomas of Walsingham's *Chronicle* [Latin] and *Ypodigma* [Latin]; at the end of the volume: 'Londini in ædibus Johannis Daij anno Dom. 1574' (folio).

(a) Latin preface by Parker
(b) Old English and Latin Alphabets
(c) Asser's *Life of Alfred* [Latin, printed in Anglo-Saxon characters, 40 pp.]
(d) The preface of Gregory's *Pastoral Care*[1] [Old English, with English interlinear and a Latin translation, 8 pp.]

The press of John Day continued for another decade, but the death of Parker within a year after the publication of the Asser checked the impulse for printing 'Saxon monuments'.[2]

The debt of Old English scholarship to Archbishop Parker cannot be indicated in the meagre list of the books put out under his editorship. His wonderful collection of manuscripts; the types he gave to Day; his encouragement and financial aid to Foxe and Lambarde; the backing of his authoritative position, and his personal enthusiasm for research, however faulty the results, make him indeed what Strype calls him, 'the chief Retriever of our Native Language'. Before his death, Parker had so organized the Church of England that there was no pressing need of Old English documents to support its policy. The legal and antiquarian interest was in the ascendancy; Lambarde was a man of such mental acuteness that his researches in Old English law satisfied the nation for nearly a century;[3] and, for fifty years,[4] antiquarian interest alone kept Old English from relapsing into oblivion. Within this interregnum, Vulcanius[5] included

---

[1] Cf. p. 20, letter of Bishop Jewel.

[2] Day printed two other editions of Foxe's *Actes and Monuments*, with Old English extracts in Anglo-Saxon type, 1576, 1583.

[3] Cf. Wheloc's edition of the Old English laws, 1643.

[4] From Parker's Asser to L'Isle's *Saxon Monuments*, 1574-1623.

[5] Vulcanius Bonaventura was the pseudonym of the printer Smetz. The author of the tract is unknown. Wülker, *Grundriss der Angelsächsischen Litteratur*, conjectures it to have been Anton Morillon, secretary to Cardinal Gravella. Cf. also the letter of Ussher to Junius (preface to *Glossarium Gothicum*, p. 14).

in his *De Literis & Lingua Getarum*[1] the preface of Gregory's *Pastoral Care*, with Latin translation from Parker's Asser. The Old English is here for the first time printed in Roman characters. Prior to this, in 1577, Raphael Holinshed inserted the Charter of William the Conqueror in his *Chronicles:*[2]

Here to fill up this page, I haue thought good to set downe the charter which the king Wil. the Conqueror graunted unto the citie of London, at the Special sute of William the Bishop of the same citie, aswel for the briefnesse thereof (and yet conteyning matter sufficient in those dayes to warrant his meaning) as also for the strangenesse of the English then in use. Williem Kyng grets Williem Bisceop & Godfred Portersan & ealle ya Burghwarn binnen hodon frencisce & Englisce frendlice, & Ic kiden eoy yeet Ic wille yeet git ben ealra weera lagayweord ye yet weeran on Eadwards daege kings and Ic will yeet aelc child by his fader yrsnume aefter his faders daege and Ic nelle ge wolian, yeet aenig man eoy aenis wrang beode, God eoy heald.

This charter is obviously a corrupt copy, but serves to illustrate how early scholars of the language confused and misapplied the term 'Saxon' to any early English writing.[3]

Hakluyt inserted some translations from Alfred's *Orosius* in the second edition of his *Voyages*, 1599. He laid no claim to any knowledge of Old English, nor did he attempt to print the original. These extracts contribute nothing to Old English scholarship, but

---

[1] Printed at Antwerp, 1597.

[2] *The Chronicles of Raphaell Holingshed* 1. 1577.

[3] The charter of William to the city of London reads as follows: 'Will'm Kyng gret Will'm bisceop and Gosfreg ⅚ portirefan and ealle þa burhwaru binnan Londone Frencisce and Englisce freondlice. and ic ky ⅚ e eow þat ic wylle þat get beon eallra þæra laga weor ⅚ e þe gyt wæran onEadwerdes dæge kynges. and ic wylle þæt ælc cyld beo his fæder yrfnume. æfter his fæderdæge. and ic nelle geþolian þat ænig man eow ænig wrang beode. god eow gehealde.' Cf. Stubbs, *Select Charters* (Oxford, 1905), p. 82.

they do indicate an interest sufficient to warrant the insertion of passages or translations in extraneous material.

There were some scholarly undertakings projected in the sixteenth century which were not printed. Lambarde evidently intended to make extensive use of the *Anglo-Saxon Chronicle*, since he transcribed it to A. D. 1001.[1] Although no Old English title-page or preface bears the names of Joscelyn or Nowell, these scholars materially advanced the study of the language. John Joscelyn (1529-1603) was a Herefordshire man, educated at Queen's College, Cambridge, where he was Latin and Greek lecturer, 1551-52. On resigning his fellowship, he became Latin secretary to Parker in 1559. Parker set him to work at collecting Old English manuscripts, many of which, with his notes, are among the Cottonian (Add. 4787); Harleian (338, 420, 692); and Royal (5. B. 15, f. 134) manuscripts in the British Museum, and the Lambeth manuscripts (585, 593). He prepared *Annales Angliæ ex variis chroniciis et historiis MSS. desumptse*,[2] and, with John Parker,[3] collected materials for an Old English dictionary,[4] which formed the basis of more elaborate glossaries in the seventeenth and eighteenth centuries. His close association with Parker, and the worth of the latter's name on a title-page, make it impossible to find out how much of the Archbishop's voluminous writings was his own, how much of it Joscelyn's. Very probably the greater portion of the *De Antiquitate Britannicæ Ecclesiæ* was Joscelyn's work. Curiously enough, Joscelyn seems never to have thought of turning the attention of

[1] This was a copy of Cott. Otho B. XI, now lost.

[2] MS. Cott. Vitell. E. XIV 2. 153.

[3] Son of the Archbishop.

[4] Bodl. MS. 33; Cott. Titus A. XV and XVI. For the dictionaries, cf. chap. II.

university students towards the Old English language, for at his death he bequeathed £100 to a Hebrew lecturer in his own college.

Laurence Nowell (d. 1576) is the earliest, and probably the most careful, of sixteenth-century 'Saxonists'. The date of his birth is uncertain, but he was a resident of Brasenose College, Oxford, about 1536, although he took his degree from Cambridge. Later he became master of a grammar-school at Sutton Coldfield in Warwickshire, suffered a period of exile under Mary, and on his return to England was made Archdeacon of Derby, and Dean of Lichfield. It is not certain just how Nowell became interested in Old English, but there is no evidence that he was under the influence of Parker. None of his labors were printed during his lifetime, but he may be justly considered as the founder of legal interest in Old English, just as Parker was the discoverer of its theological bearings. His early knowledge of the Lancashire dialect, his experience as a schoolmaster, and his knowledge of whatever Low Dutch he may have learned during his exile, would peculiarly fit him for the investigation of the early English language. He became acquainted with Lambarde through his brother, Robert Nowell, attorney-general of the Court of Wards in Gray's Inn. The intimacy was mutually helpful, the scholar imparting to Lambarde a rudimentary knowledge of Old English, and in turn being instructed in the legal significance of the manuscripts he was collecting. There is a tradition that Alexander Nowell[1] was a roommate of Foxe, the martyrologist, in Brasenose College. The mutual acquaintance of the Nowells with Foxe and Lambarde may have first brought the young lawyer to the notice of Parker. In addition to the collection of laws published by Lambarde, Nowell compiled a

---

[1] Dean of St. Paul's, elder brother of Laurence.

Vocabularium Saxonicum[1], which passed successively
to Lambarde, Somner, and Selden, and finally into the
keeping of the Bodleian library.

Briefly, then, the most lasting contribution of the
sixteenth century to Old English scholarship consisted
in the manuscript collections. Active interest in the
language grew out of the Reformation in the latter
third of the century, and subsided with the readjust-
ment of civil and ecclesiastical life under Queen Elizabeth. The actual contributions in print extend over
little more than ten years, and consist of a few homilies of Ælfric, Alfred's translation of the Latin preface
to Gregory's *Pastoral Care*, a collection of laws,
and an Old English version of the Gospels. To these
may be added a few extracts from the *Textus Roffensis*, and stray quotations from the *Anglo-Saxon
Chronicle*, and from deeds and charters. The principal contributions are to be found within the compass
of four books.[2] The workers may be reduced to Nowell,
Joscelyn, and Lambarde. Parker had a great man's
genius for making others work; the very nature of early
editions shows how mechanical was the editing of Old
English manuscripts. This routine-work Parker very
likely turned over to his scholarly secretary, supervis-
ing perhaps, and most certainly encouraging, the efforts
of all engaged in 'Saxon' studies. The results of Nowell's labor show in what Lambarde accomplished. As
for Foxe, although his name attaches to the edition

[1] MS. Seld. Arch B. For the use of this, cf. chap. II. Nowell
also left: 'Codex chartaceus in Quarto, partim per Guil. Lambardum, partim per Laurent. Nowellum ex Cod. antiquis descriptus, in quo occurrunt
Saxonice' . . . (Cott. Vesp. A. V.); and 'Excerpta quædam Saxonica',
A. D. 189-997, and 'Excerpta', A. D. 1043-1079 (Cott. Dom. A. xviii).

[2] *A Testimonie of Antiquitie*, 1563 (Ælfric's Homilies). *Archaionomia*,
1568 (Anglo-Saxon laws). *The Fower Gospels*, 1571 (Scripture in the vernacular). Asser's *Ælfredi Regis Res Gestæ*, 1574 (Alfred's translation of
Gregory's *Pastoral Care*).

of the Gospels, it is unlikely that he had anything to do with the Old English portions of the book.   That all the results were crude was due not only to the meagre knowledge of the language, but also to the customary careless methods of the age.   With printed books little more than a century in existence, exact scholarship in any field was not to be expected, and it would be unfair to judge the scholarship of the period by our present-day standards.   All those interested in Old English were, with the exception of Lambarde, Oxford and Cambridge men, and in the thick of Reformation-troubles.   It was, in all instances, as men of affairs, and not as collegians, that they gave the world the fruits of their studies.   Since 'Saxon' learning did not pass into the hands of the universities until well into the seventeenth century, we may characterize the Old English scholarship of the sixteenth century as uncritical, controversial, and non-academic.

CHAPTER II

The Growth of Old English Scholarship in the Seventeenth Century

The seventeenth century witnessed the gradual absorption of the study of Old English by the universities, resulting in the foundation of a lecture in the language, and in the publication of a dictionary.

It has been generally assumed that interest in Old English lapsed during the half century between the death of Parker and the publication of L'Isle's *Saxon Treatise*.[1] This is not the case, for the interregnum is filled with efforts which contributed to the preservation and growth of Old English studies. The revival of Old English might have come to an end with the death of its great sixteenth-century patron, but for the Society of Antiquaries. This Society was a natural outgrowth of Parker's enthusiasm for national monuments; it began in 1572, and continued many years as a private organization, under the patronage of Sir Robert Cotton. In 1589 the Society petitioned Queen Elizabeth for the use of some public building as a place of meeting, and for the housing of a library. The petition discloses the object of the Society to have been the preservation of manuscripts and rare books relating to English history and antiquities, and the study of modern languages.[2] During the troubles of the civil wars, the Society of Antiquaries temporarily lapsed, but it had already acted as a lever to raise the study of English antiquities to something like the plane

[1] 1575-1623.   [2] Cf. Appendix IV.

42

of the classics, which had so long monopolized the interest of the universities.

William Camden's passion for antiquities of every kind led him to include some specimens of Old English in his *Anglica, Normannica . . . scripta.*[1] Two years later, in *Remaines of a greater worke concerning Britaine,*[2] he printed two versions of the Lord's Prayer in Old English.[3] To these versions he added three others, illustrating the language in the times of Henry II, Henry III, and Richard II.[4] This was the first attempt made at a comparative study of the different stages of the language. A chapter on language, names, and surnames, contains some very crude Old English etymologies.[5] A few months later, Richard Verstegan published *A Restitution of Decayed Intelligence,*[6] containing the first printed collection of meanings and etymologies of Old English words arranged in alphabetical order. The book consists of ten chapters, treating of the Saxons in Germany, their habits of life, and

[1] 'Anglica, Normannica, Hibernica, Cambrica, a veteribvs scripta: ex quibus Asser Meneuensis, Anonymus de vita Guilielmi Conquestores, Thomas Walsingham, Thomas de la More, Gulielmus Gemiticensis, Geraldus Cambrensis. Plerique nunc primum in lucem editi, ex Bibliotheca Gvilielmi Camdeni . . . Francofvrti, impensis Claudij Marnij & hæredum Johannis Aubrij Anno M. D. ciii' (folio). The specimen of Old English (pp. 25-27) is the Preface to Gregory's *Pastoral Care,* taken from Parker's Asser, with interlinear English and a Latin translation.

[2] 'Remaines of a greater worke, concerning Britaine, the inhabitants there of, their Languages, Names, Surnames, Empresses, wise Speeches, Poesies, and Epitaphs.' London, 1605. New editions, 1614, 1623, 1629, 1636, 1657, 1674.

[3] From the Durham Book.

[4] Wycliffe's translation.

[5] Cf. Lambarde, *Perambulation of Kent,* 1576; and Leland's collections, to which Camden is indebted.

[6] *A Restitution of Decayed Intelligence: In antiquities concerning the most noble and renowned English nation. By the Studie and trauaile of R. V.* Printed at Antwerp by Robert Bruney, 1605 (quarto). Subsequent editions were printed in London, 1628, 1634, 1655.

their arrival in Britain. The author discourses on the antiquity of the English tongue, tracing it to Teutonic sources, and in some instances showing how words of French origin have replaced the Old English. He also deals with the etymology of Old English proper names, of English, Saxon, Danish, and Norman family-names, ancient titles of honor, dignity, office, and contempt. One comment of Verstegan is illuminating as to the state of philological study on the Continent at the beginning of the seventeenth century:

> If in some of the etymologies of our ancient names or woords I may appeer to differ from some of the Germans that have written of the lyke, it is where I have manifestly found them to haue been mistaken, for such as thereof haue written in Germanie, haue looked but little further then vnto the language vsed among themselues, and such as in the Neetherlands haue written, haue in lyke sorte had regard vnto their only vsed speech, whereas indeed, the vnderstanding of the Teutonic vsed of our Saxon Ancestors as also that of the ancient Francks is most requisite & there unto the present; High, Low, and Eastlandish Teutonic, together with respect vnto the dependent Danish and Swedish, besydes our modern vulgar English.

Very little is known of Verstegan's personal history except that he was born in London, and, according to Wood,[1] educated at Oxford; that he was persecuted as a Catholic; that he spent much time in Antwerp; and that he died about 1634. His work is more scientific than Camden's, and, if it had appeared before the *Remains,* would doubtless have had greater popularity.[2] As it is, *A Restitution of Decayed Intelligence* marks an important advance in the work of Old English scholar-

---

[1] *Athenæ Oxonienses.*

[2] Wood comments on the fact that the numerous woodcuts by the author 'advantaged the sale of it much.'

ship, and may be considered as a forerunner of Somner's dictionary.

There was no direct contribution to the printing of Old English manuscripts in the seventeenth century before 1623;[1] for this reason, William L'Isle (1579?-1637) may be called the first Old English editor of the century. L'Isle was an Eton and Cambridge man, related to Sir Henry Spelman. A strong desire to learn the doctrinal position of the early church led him to study Old English. The only published result of this study was *A Saxon Treatise concerning the Old and New Testament*.[2] L'Isle found this manuscript of Ælfricus Grammaticus, whom he wrongly identified with Bishop Ælfric, in the library of Sir Robert Cotton.[3] The preface to his book is one of the most interesting documents

---

[1] Cf. editions of Lambarde's *Eirenarcha*, 1602, 1607, 1614, 1619; Parker's *De Antiquitate Britannicæ Ecclesiæ*, 1605 (Hanover); Foxe's *Actes and Monuments*, 1610; Selden's *Janus Anglorum*, 1610, *Titles of Honour*, 1614, *History of Tithes*, 1618. These printed fragments or passages of Old English are mostly to be found in sixteenth-century books. Marq. Freheri *Decalogi, Orationis, Symboli, Saxonica versio vetustissima*, 1610, is a reprint from *A Testimonie*, in Roman characters.

[2] 'A Saxon Treatise concerning the Old and New Testament. Written abovt the time of King Edgar (700 yeares agoe) by Ælfricvs Abbas, thought to be the same that was afterward Archbishop of Canterbvrie. Whereby Appeares what was the Canon of holy Scripture here then receiued, and that the Church of England had it so long agoe in her Mother-tongue. Now first pvblished in print with English of our times, by William L'isle of Wilbvrgham, Esquier for the Kings Bodie: The Originall remaining still to be seene in Sr Robert Cottons Librarie, at the end of his lesser Copie of the Saxon Pentatevch. And Herevnto is added ovt of the Homilies and Epistles of the fore-said Ælfricvs, a second Edition of A Testimonie of Antiquitie &c, touching the Sacrament of the Bodie and Blovd of the Lord, here publikely preached and receiued in the Saxons time', &c. . . . London: Printed by John Haviland for Henrie Seile, 1623. In 1638 the book was re-issued with a different title-page: 'Divers Ancient Monuments in the Saxon Tongue', &c. London, printed by E. G. for Frances Eglesfield. There is a slight difference in the order of arrangement of the contents, but no evidence of a new edition. The title-page may be spurious.

[3] Now MS. Bodl. Laud E. 19.

connected with the development of Old English scholarship.[1] It gives an account of how an early student
gained some knowledge of the language without the
aid of grammars or dictionaries. First he acquainted
himself with High and Low Dutch; then he began to
read all the books and manuscripts he could find in
archaic English, observing that the older they were,
the nearer they seemed to approach the 'Saxon'. In
the course of this reading he came upon Gavin Doug-
las' Scottish translation of Virgil. He found it very
difficult, but mastered it by the help of the Latin. Next
he read the work of Freher. So far, he had not attempted anything in the Anglo-Saxon character, of
which he made some study before undertaking *A Testimonie*, the *Fower Gospels*, and such scraps of Old English as he could find in print, or in old charters and
record-books. Being then able, as he says, 'to swim
without bladders', he began to investigate the manuscript collections of Cotton, Spelman, and Cambridge
University. In his *Saxon Treatise*, L'Isle proved himself a good translator for his day; he purposed further
publications of Old English texts,[2] especially of the
Gospels, but these were never printed. L'Isle's great
enthusiasm for the beauty and flexibility of the English language rises to poetic fervor in his preface:

> Our language is improued above all others now
> spoken by any nation, and become the fairest, the
> nimblest, the fullest; most apt to vary the phrase, most
> ready to receiue good composition, most adorned with
> sweet words and sentences, with witty Quips and ouer-
> ruling Prouerbes: yea, able to expresse any hard con-
> ceit whatsoever with great dexterity: . . . but sure
> to neglect the beginnings of such an excellent tongue,

[1] Cf. Appendix II.

[2] Bodl. MSS. Laud E. 33 and Laud D. 85 contain Ælfric's translation
of the Pentateuch, Joshua, Judges, Job, and the Psalter, from which L'Isle
intended to print. Cf. *Anglia* 30. 105ff.

will bring vpon vs the foule disgrace not onely of ignorance, . . . but of extreme ingratitude towards
our famous ancestors, who left vs so many, so goodly
monuments in their old Dialect recorded.[1]

The next publication bearing on Old English
studies was a law-encyclopædia, printed in 1626 by Sir
Henry Spelman, under the title of *Archæologus*.[2] Spelman (1564?-1641) was a worthy successor to Parker
as a patron of Old English. A great collector of manuscripts, a member of the Society of Antiquaries, the
promotor of L'Isle's publication, the founder of a
'Saxon' lecture at Cambridge—he was more than a
patron of such learning: he was a laborious student of
the language, and an extensive editor of his own re-

---

[1] Cf. Appendix II. L'Isle's conception of dexterity led him to compose
very poor verse. Ritson ascribes to him some stanzas signed W. L., prefixed to Bk. 3 of Spenser's *Faerie Queene*. He prefixes a dedicatory poem
of thirty-nine stanzas to his *Saxon Treatise*. The verses are intended as
an imitation of Virgil's *Fourth Eclogue*. Stanzas 32 and 33 may serve to
show how a good prose writer was a bad poet:

> As long as *Brittaine* bears you Shepherds stout,
> As well for warre, if need be, as to keepe
> Your flocks within, and beasts of rauine out;
> As long as wooll grows on the backs of sheepe;
> As Corn, Salt, Lead, Tin, Hides, Cloth, Silu'r & Woad,
> Your Kingdoms loaden at home discharge abroad:
> As long as Castles built of Pitch and Wood,
> Shall *Delos*-like about your Island float,
> To bring-in, and beare-out what seemes you good;
> Though nothing bring they but we might forget,
> Tobacco, Puppets, Hobby horses, Silke.

[2] 'Archæologus in Modum Glossarii ad rem antiquam posteriorem, con-
tinentis Latino Barbara peregrina obsoleta, et Novatæ Significationis
Vocabula, quae post labefactatas a Gothis Vandalisq; res Europæas; in
Ecclesiasticis profanisq; Scriptoribus; variarum item Gentium legibus
antiquis, Chartis et Formulis occurrunt. Scholiis et Commentariis illustrata in quibus prisci Ritus quam plurimi; Magistratus; Dignitates, Munera,
Officia, Mores, Leges, et consuetudines enarrantur. Londini, apud Johan-
nem Beale, 1626.'

Only 1 A-L, appeared in 1626; complete edition by Dugdale, 1664;
third edition, 1687.

searches.   It is true, as his biographer says,[1] that he was in middle life when he settled down to 'books and learned men', but we can hardly accept Aubrey's statement that his 'witts opened late', or that 'he was an indifferent Latin student in youth',[2] for Spelman was a Cambridge man, a composer of Latin verses, and a member of Lincoln's Inn.[3]   The interruption to his studies was a business litigation that lasted fifteen years.[4]   In 1612 he took up his residence at Westminster, in order to be near the Cotton library.   His long experience with lawsuits had greatly interested him in the origin of English laws,[5] on which subject he purposed compiling a book from original records. In the course of his reading he found so much difficulty in assigning meanings to Old English and Latin law-terms, that he determined to make a serious study of Old English.   Having done this, he compiled a glossary of Old English and Latin law-terms, the *Archæologus*. In this undertaking he was encouraged by Ussher, Selden, Laud, and Cotton.   The first part, to the letter L, completed in 1619, was offered to Bill, the king's printer, for five pounds' worth of books.   The offer was refused, and Spelman finally bore the expense of publication, 1626.   The book had little sale, and Spelman did not get rid of the copies until 1637.   In the meantime he met William Dugdale, to whom he gave much help

[1] Gibson, *Life of Spelman*, 1723.

[2] John Aubrey, *Lives of Eminent Literary Men*.

[3] 1586.

[4] Spelman purchased Blockborough Nunnery, Middleton Parish, Norfolk, in 1594.   This involved him in a series of lawsuits which lasted until 1611.

[5] One of the first results of his study was an essay, prepared in 1614 for the Society of Antiquaries, on the *Antiquity and Etymology of the Law Terms in England*, published, London. 1684, as *Discourses of Law Terms*. This deals with the law-terms of the Jews, Greeks, Romans, Saxons, and Normans.

and encouragement. Some twenty years after Spelman's death, Dugdale[1] edited the second volume of the glossary; it appeared, with a new edition of the first volume, in 1664.[2] Dugdale has been accused of taking great liberties with Spelman's papers, but the printed copies do not materially differ from the extant portions of the manuscript.[3] The expense of the complete edition was defrayed by a subscription,[4] contributed to by Lord Chancellor Hyde, Gilbert Sheldon, Thomas Barlow,[5] and many other churchmen and gentlemen. Various reasons are assigned for Spelman's failure to print the whole of the work. A story long current declared that Archbishop Laud was so scandalized at certain explanations of *Magna Charta* and *Magnum Concilium* that he refused to license the second volume. Gibson thought that the great cost of printing, family burdens, and the unremunerative character of the work, deterred Spelman from completing it in later life. Another possible reason lies in his absorption in the *Concilia, Decreta, Leges.* His interest in the origin of English law had led him to extensive reading in ecclesiastical laws and the history of the Middle Ages. As a result, be began in 1630 a compilation on the councils, decrees, laws, and constitutions of the English Church.[6] In this undertaking, Spelman had the co-operation of his son, John

[1] The manuscript was in the possession of Spelman's grandson, Charles, and the editorship was assumed by Dugdale at the request of Archbishop Sheldon and Lord Clarendon. The proportion of Old English words in the entire glossary is small.

[2] This was the second book ever reviewed in the *Journal des Sçavans* (Jan. 5, 1665).

[3] Part of the manuscript was lost before it came to the Bodleian. The printed copies tally with the manuscript as far as *Riota.*

[4] The total subscription amounted to £316.13.4.

[5] Provost of Queen's College, Oxford.

[6] Cf. Parker, *De Antiquitate Britannicæ Ecclesiæ*, 1572.

4

Spelman, and of Jeremy Stephens,[1] and the patronage of Laud and Ussher. Only the first volume appeared in the author's lifetime.[2]

John Spelman (1594-1643) was heir both to his father's antiquarian collections and to his literary tastes. He was a Cambridge man, a member of Gray's Inn, and an extensive traveler in France and Italy, where he became acquainted with some of the leading scholars. While the king was residing in Oxford, he summoned John Spelman as a member of his privy council; he took up his residence at Brasenose College, and there, presumably, compiled a life of King Alfred, which was not published until 1678.[3]   It was the plan of Sir Henry to have his son compile an Old English grammar, but this too was frustrated by the death of both men within two years of each other. John Spelman's one great contribution to Old English publica-

[1] Jeremy Stephens (1592-1664), an Oxford man, native of Shropshire. He edited Spelman's work on *Tithes*, 1647. It is said that he went to Cambridge with Spelman, to transcribe Old English manuscripts, and that it was at this period that the Anglo-Saxon lectureship was conceived.

[2] 'Concilia, decreta, leges, constitutiones, in re ecclesiarum orbis Britannici. Viz. Pambritannica, Pananglica, Scotica, Hibernica, Cambrica, Mannica, Provincialia, Diocesana. Ab initio Christianæ ibidem religionis, ad nostram usque ætatem. Uti reperiuntur in eorundem Actis, Canonibus, Ecclesiasticis, Regnorum Constitutionibus, Senatus Consultis, Principum Rescriptis, Libris impressis, et antique MSS. in regnum etiam priscorum Diplomatibus, Chartis, Schedis, et Monumentis veteribus studiose congesta. Opera et scrutinio Henrici Spelmann, Eq. Aur. Tribus distincta tomis: quorum, Primus hic tomus ea continet, quæ a primis Christi seculis, usque ad introitum Normannorum (id est, an. Dom. 1066) habita sunt et celebrata. Londini, excudebat Richardus Badger' . . . 1639. fol. Complete edition 1664, Dugdale. Volume 2 begins at the Conquest. Dugdale asserted that only 57 sheets of the 200 in the volume were Spelman's work. Most of the edition was burned in the great fire of London.

[3] John Spelman died of camp-fever while at Oxford. Christopher Ware translated the life into Latin, and it was printed at Oxford in 1678, with a commentary by Obadiah Walker. Hearne re-edited it in 1709, leaving out Walker's additions.

tions was an edition of the Psalter, 1640.[1] This is the first scholarly edition of an Old English text with collations.[2] The volume consists of a short dedication to Archbishop Laud; a preface to the reader;[3] and the text, Old English and Latin interlinear, with variants collated in the margin.

By means of his two great works, the *Archæologus* and the *Concilia*, Henry Spelman became a founder of scientific philology and of church-history.[4] These, with his establishment of the Cambridge lecture, give him great prominence in the development of Old English studies. It was through his own difficulties in research that Spelman came to realize how little was known of the language;[5] but not until he was advanced in years did this realization bear fruit. In 1630 he began collecting materials for the *Concilia*, and spent some time in Cambridge, where he had taken Jeremy Stephens to transcribe manuscripts.[6] It was at this

[1] 'Psalterium Davidis Latino-Saxonicum vetus. A Johanne Spelmanno D. Hen. fil. editum. E vetustissimo exemplari Ms. in Bibliotheca ipsius Henrici, & cum tribus aliis non multo minus vetustis collatum. Londini, excudebat R. Badger.' 1640. 4°.

[2] The manuscripts used for collating were from the Cambridge Library, Trinity College, Cambridge, and the Arundel collection.

[3] In this preface he emphasizes the fact that image-worship was not historical in the English church: 'Tum ut librum ipsum fideliter recitemus tum ut antiquioris Ecclesiæ Anglicanæ praxin sinceram ob oculos ponamus, quæ sub illo tempore (ut videtur) nec beatorum animas, nec beatissimam Virginem *Mariam*, nec crucem Domini, adorandas docuit.'

[4] David Wilkins re-edited the *Concilia*, expanding it into four volumes, 1736. This is the direct basis of Stubbs' *Councils and Ecclesiastical Documents*, 1869-73.

[5] 'Paulatim ita exhalavit animam nobile illud majorum nostrorum & pervetustum idioma; ut in universo (quod sciam) orbe, ne unus hodie reperiatur, qui hoc sciti perfective calleat. Pauci quidam qui vel exoletas literas usquequaque noverint.'—Spelman, preface to the *Archæologus*.

[6] D'Ewes asserted that when he met Spelman in 1630 he was blind and very old. This cannot be true, since he was just beginning the collections for his great work.

time, probably, that the Old English lectureship first
suggested itself to him. He succeeded in interesting
Abraham Wheloc (1593-1653), Professor of Arabic at
Cambridge, in his plan. Wheloc is said to have spent
seven years in mastering Old English, in order to fit
himself for the office that Spelman designed. Spelman's
idea was to further the study of the language by lectures and by publications. Apparently no lectures
were ever given on this foundation. The reason is not
far to seek. The promoters of the scheme saw the
futility of instruction without a grammar or a dictionary. Until these were supplied, the obvious thing
was to publish the most interesting and useful manuscripts. The situation is made quite clear in the
following letter:

Mr. Wheelock:

I gave my Lord of Ely[1] thanks in your behalfe and
moved also for the continuance of his favor about the
Lyvinge you ayme at, and for that, he answered that
he had directed you the course for obteyning it to Dr.
Cosens.[2] I also moved him about our desired Lecture
of domestique Antiquities touching our Church and
reviving the Saxon tongue, which he well approveth
and desireth to farther, but by all meanes he would
that there should be first a Grammar and a Dictionary
of that tongue published. I tould him that I so en-
tended, and that my sonne,[3] after the Psalter finished,
should put forth the Grammar[4] which I had by me.
And for the Dictionary, Mr. de Laet[5] of Leiden in the
Low Countries is very busy about one, and to that
purpose hath written three letters unto me. I am not
willing that it should be done by a stranger, and we
here (to whome it more particularly belongeth) be pre-

[1] Matthew Wren.

[2] John Cosin, Bishop of Durham; Vice Chancellor of Cambridge, 1639.

[3] John Spelman.

[4] Possibly Nowell's vocabulary.

[5] Jean de Laet, born Antwerp 1593, died Leyden 1649, geographer and
philologist.

termitted. I have therefore written to him, that we have here in England some Dictionaries MS. already of very good use, done by skillful men in that language, and many other Collections by other men, all which I endeavour to get drawn into one Body; and that the worke may be more compleat, have desired his conjectanea and association in the business, he being a very apt man for it in respect for his naturall tongue and former travail in matters of antiquity.[1] I have yet received no answer from him, but suggest an hope unto myself, to have somewhat done in this next Springe, desireing your leisure may then permit you to assist it. And that in the mean tyme you would applie your self to the antientest Authors of our Church and Church History, and my desire is to present the World with usefull and disired worthies. And before we make to mutch noyes of it, we must, like prudent Buylders, consider and resolve of the Platt and Fabrick of our purpose, what it shall be, how prosecuted and supported afterward, for we must not launch out into the deep before we know the points of our compass, and the port wherat we hope to aryve. My strength is not lyke my mynde. I send you herewith as you desire Aelfrics MS. Grammar, and thus commit you and all to God as

Your very loveing friend
Henry Spelman

Barbacan[2] 28 Sept.
  1638.

Spelman founded his lecture in 1639—£10 salary and the living of Middleton,[3] worth about £50 a year —but formal recognition by the University was not granted before 1640.[4] It is evident that the grammar

---

[1] De Laet gave up his project, which was taken up by Sir Symonds D'Ewes.

[2] The London residence of Spelman's son-in-law.

[3] 'The place is hard by Lynn, and you may every week goe or send between it and Cambridge on Munday mornings'.—Letter of Spelman to Wheloc (Harl. MS. 7041).

[4] Cf. Appendix I, Wheloc to D'Ewes and Spelman to Wheloc, Nos. 3, 4.

and dictionary were deferred in favor of the publication of historical documents. As a result, Wheloc brought out an edition of Bede's *Ecclesiastical History*,[1] with portions of the *Anglo-Saxon Chronicle*, 1643. These were reissued the next year, together with an enlarged edition of Lambarde's *Archaionomia*.[2] In the preface Wheloc states that Archbishop Ussher had recommended him for the 'Saxon' lecture, and had suggested obtaining knowledge of the language by reading the 'Saxon' Gospels. He greatly praises the scholarship of Jeremy Stephens, and mentions how Spelman, finding so much material in Corpus Christi library, had partly determined to found the lecture. Wheloc's contribution to the Old English scholarship of his century is important. Bede's *Ecclesiastical History* alone would have been a notable achievement; together with the *Anglo-Saxon Chronicle*,[3] it gives him

[1] 'Historiæ Ecclesiasticæ Gentis Anglorum Libri V. a Venerabili Beda Presbytero scripti: tribus præcipue MSS Latinis, a mendis haud paucis repurgati: ab augustissimo veterum Anglo-Saxonum Rege Aluredo (sive Alfredo) examinati; ejusque paraphrasi Saxonica eleganter explicati; tribus nunc etiam MSS Saxonicis collati; Una cum annotationibus & analectis e publicis Veteris Ecclesiæ Anglicanæ Homiliis aliisque MSS Saxonicis hinc inde excerptis, nec antea Latine datis: quibus in calce operis Saxonicam Chronologiam seriem hujus imprimis Historiæ complectentem nunquam antea in lucem editam, nunc quoque primo Latine versam contexuimus: Opera hæc fere omnia Saxonica hactenus in archivis recondita, nunc demum in Reipublicæ Literariæ usum deprompta e Bibliotheca Publica Cantabrigiensis quibus accesserunt Anglo-Saxonicæ Leges: Et ultimo Leges Henrici 1. nunc primum editæ Cantabrigiæ ex officina Rogeri Daniel celeberrimæ Accademinæ Typographc. MDCXLIII.' The university purchased Anglo-Saxon type for printing Wheloc's works. Cf. Appendix III.

[2] Wheloc added laws of William the Conqueror, Henry I, and the Canons of Edgar and Ælfric.

[3] Wheloc used the following manuscripts of the *Anglo-Saxon Chronicle:* Cott. MS. Otho B, XI, collated with C. C. C. C. MS. CLXXIII. These were but a few of the available copies; cf. Bodl. MS. Laud 636; transcripts of Cott. Tib. A. VI and Dom. A. VIII, used by Gibson, 1692: cf. Cott. Tib. B. 1 and Cott. Tib. B. IV, used by Ingram, 1823. Somner made a transcript of Cott. Tib. B. 1.

the distinction of making accessible in print the two most important historical documents of the English language.[1] The deaths of Henry and John Spelman at the very outset of the Cambridge activities in Old English, together with the turmoil of the civil war, soon rendered the lectureship inopportune; yet there were enough persons interested in the success of Old English studies to urge the appointment of another incumbent at Wheloc's death in 1653.

At this time a combination of circumstances altered the trend of university studies in Old English, and rather abruptly transferred the activities from Cambridge to Oxford. The choice of a new incumbent fell to Sir Henry Spelman's grandson, Roger, and he designated the Rev. Samuel Foster for the Middleton living. At the same time, the friends of William Somner were urging his appointment, both because of his knowledge of the language and in order to further the publication of his Old English dictionary. Apparently Roger Spelman did not know Somner, but was willing to give him the lectureship. The result was that the benefaction was divided, and, to all intents and purposes, Cambridge ceased to promote Old English studies[2] until the scholarly world at large took up the study in the nineteenth century.

The correspondence of literary men in the seventeenth century indicates how they felt the need of grammars and dictionaries to advance the study of Old English.[3] The exodus of scholars to the Nether-

---

[1] Gerard Langbaine (1609-1659), Provost of Queen's College, Oxford, projected an edition of the *Anglo-Saxon Chronicle*, but was anticipated by Wheloc.

[2] The deaths of the two elder Spelmans, the sequestration of their estate, the troubles of the civil war, as well as the division of stipend and living, resulted in this decline.

[3] Cf. Appendix I.

lands in the reign of Mary had created an interest in
Germanic dialects; yet Old English philology developed
very slowly, chiefly because of the persistency with
which English scholars clung to Latin as a medium of
interpreting their own language. The growth of a
dictionary is a slow process, and in the ninety-three
years intervening between the first Old English text
edited by Parker and the appearance of Somner's
dictionary, there had been various attempts at compiling vocabularies of the language. First among these
attempts were the sixteenth-century manuscript vocabularies of John Parker and John Joscelyn, and that of
Laurence Nowell.[1] These compilers based their work
on the Latin-Old English vocabulary of Ælfric, attached to his Latin grammar.[2] Both were mere fragments. In print before Somner's dictionary were the
Rerum et verborum explicatio of Lambarde's *Archaionomia;* the scattered etymologies in *A Perambulation
of Kent* and in Camden's *Remains;* the more ambitious
classified lists in Verstegan's *Restitution of Decayed Intelligence;* the incidental glossing of Old English words
in Minsheu's *Guide into Tongues,* in Spelman's *Archæologus,* in Wat's edition of Matthew Paris, and in
Casaubon's *De Quatuor Linguis Commentationes.* Somner himself had attempted a glossary, which appears
at the end of Twysden's *Historiæ Anglicanæ Scriptores
X,* as 'Glossarium in quo obscuriora quæque vocabula
quæ toto hoc opere continentur'. De Laet, the Dutch
scholar, had begun a dictionary, but was halted by
Spelman in favor of a projected work by D'Ewes and
Wheloc. D'Ewes never got further in his undertaking than the transcribing of the Joscelyn-Parker vo-

---

[1] The Joscelyn-Parker vocabulary was apparently collected from the
Gospels; Nowell's vocabulary was mostly from the laws he had gathered.

[2] For the Ælfric Grammar, cf. chap. III.

cabulary, and some unmethodized notes gathered in the course of his antiquarian browsings.[1]

The most ambitious philological undertaking before the Somner dictionary was the *Guide into Tongues*, 1617. This dictionary of eleven languages[2] was completed in 1610. The struggles of its author, John Minsheu,[3] in trying to finish and publish his work, illustrate some of the difficulties that beset a seventeenth-century lexicographer.[4] Several times he was brought to a standstill through lack of money. For a time he worked at Cambridge; later he migrated to Oxford with his helpers, and spent four months revising his dictionary, with the aid of Oxford students. The help granted him by the University was his 'first comfort', as he had spent all he had, and was heavily in debt. After many efforts, he succeeded in getting letters patent from the king, but on the presentation of these, with the copy, to the Company of Stationers, he was refused, because of his debts. Minsheu next petitioned the Societies of Gray's Inn and of Lincoln's Inn; with their contributions, he was enabled to begin printing. Later he had aid from the Inns of Court and the Inner Temple; among private people, he had considerable help from Sir Henry Spelman and Henry Brigges,[5] to whom he dedicated his work. From Cambridge he

[1] Simonds D'Ewes (1602-1650) was a typical antiquary, corresponding with most of the noted scholars of his day; collecting, transcribing, planning many things, but never publishing any direct contributions to Old English scholarship. He published *Journals of all the Parliaments during the Reign of Queen Elizabeth;* and his *Autobiography* (printed 1845) gives much incidental information about Old English scholars.

[2] The second edition omits Portuguese and Welsh.

[3] John Minsheu (fl. 1617) was a professor of languages, living for the most part in London. His poverty was a great hindrance to his ambitious undertakings.

[4] Cf. his Epistle to the Reader, prefixed to the dictionary.

[5] Probably the mathematician (1561-1630).

had a number of subscribers,[1] and from Oxford a letter
commending his dictionary as 'a rare & excellent work,
pleasant and profitable'.[2] As the title indicates, the
book is an elaborate attempt at comparative etymology,[3] and is the first general dictionary to take cog-
nizance of Old English.

Curiously enough, Somner migrated from Cambridge to Oxford, with his dictionary, just fifty years
after Minsheu. Although Cambridge had given Somner the stipend of the 'Saxon lecture', the University
was not in a position to advance the publication of his
dictionary, because of its precarious state in the civil
war, and because its Anglo-Saxon types were too large
for his purpose.[4] Oxford was practically untouched by
the war, and, as it had recently acquired Anglo-Saxon
types of the proper size, arrangements were made to
publish the dictionary there. Like most phases of
early 'Saxon' scholarship, the production of the dictionary grew out of an enterprise but slightly connected with Old English. William Somner (1598-

[1] The original price of the dictionary was 22 shillings; this was one of
the first books published by subscription.

[2] The Oxford testimony is dated Nov. 10, 1610, and signed by John
King, Vice-Chancellor; Leon Hutten, Dep. Vice Chan.; R. Kilby, Col.
Linc. Rec.; John Williams, Prin. Jesus; R. Kettle, Pres. Trin.; John Breck-
eridge, Pres. S. Johns; Geo. Ryves, Warden New Coll.; John Spenser, Pres.
Corpus Christi.

[3] 'The Guide into Tongues, with their agreement and consent one with
another, as also their etymology; that is, the Reasons and Derevations of
all or the most part of wordes in these nine languages, viz. English, Low
Dutch, High Dutch, French, Italian, Spanish, Latine, Greek, Hebrew;
also the exposition of the Termes of the Lawes of this Land, drawn from
their originall the Saxon and Norman Tongues, with the description of the
Magistracies, Offices and Officers and Titles of Dignities . . . By the
Industrie, Studie, Labour and at the Charges of John Minsheu.'—1617;
second edition, 1625, folio, pp. 759.

A 'Saxon' alphabet is 'set down for the Readers use, to reade the Saxon
wordes, often times in this Dictionary used.'

[4] The Cambridge types were Great Primer. Cf. Appendix III.

1669), when of age for the University, was made clerk to his father in the ecclesiastical court of Canterbury. Here, through the help of Archbishop Laud, he first had access to old records. His chief interest being in classic historians, his first publication was, quite naturally, a history of the antiquities of Canterbury, 1640, dedicated to Laud. In this he acknowledged help from Meric Casaubon. Thus far Somner had searched only Latin writers and records since the Conquest. 'There is', says White Kennett, 'a sacred ambition in the spirit of Learning that will not let a man rest without new conquer'd and enlarg'd dominions'.[1] Fired with this spirit, Somner undertook the study of Old English, being urged on by Casaubon, who says that while lamenting the ignorance of 'Saxon' and its remains, he met Somner, whose ability and enthusiasm led him to incite the young man to study the language. Casaubon further promised him help, and any materials he could furnish.[2]

It is impossible to trace Somner's achievements in Old English without some mention of Casaubon, who was born at Geneva about 1599, and having come to England as a youth, received his degree from Christ Church, Oxford,[3] and gained a great reputation for extensive learning. Wood rather sarcastically remarks that 'he was a general scholar but not extraordinary in any one sort, unless in criticisms'.[4]

Somner gained a knowledge in Teutonic languages while a student of Old English, and was considered so proficient in German that Casaubon, who desired to use an epistle of Justus Lipius containing a long list

[1] White Kennett, *Life of Somner*, prefixed to *Roman Forts and Ports*, 1693.

[2] Casaubon, *De Quatuor Linguis*, p. 140.

[3] M. A., Oxford, 1621.

[4] Wood, *Athenæ Oxonienses*.

of old German words, which he thought had affinity
to Old English, sent his manuscript to Somner, to get
his opinion. The resulting comments by Somner were
too lengthy to be inserted in Casaubon's essay, so he
added them as an appendix to his *De Quatuor Linguis.*[1]
This appendix bears the title, 'Gulielmi Somneri Cantuariensis ad verba vetera Germanica a V. Cl. Justo
Lipsio Epist. Cent. III, ad Belgas Epist. XLIV, col-
lecta, Notæ'. Curiously enough, although he saw the
strong affinity of Old English and German, Casaubon
made a vigorous effort to connect 'Saxon' with Greek.[2]
Casaubon's scholarship was so highly esteemed that
Cromwell offered him a large sum to write a history of
the civil war; this offer was refused, as was the government of the Swedish universities. His contribution tc
Old English scholarship lies in the encouragement that
he gave to Somner, rather than in his own publications.

The circumstances that ultimately led to the Old
English dictionary, 1659, may be traced in some extracts from Somner's biography:[3]

It was an observation of the learned, that no one
nation had so many and various Histories of their own
affairs, as that of England, which it would be justice
and mercy to redeem, and expose to view. The proposal was made by that industrious Bookseller, Cor-
nelius Bee, who about 1641 had importun'd Sir Roger
Twysden to supply him with materials of this kind for
the press.

With the help of Ussher and Selden, ten English historians were transcribed from manuscripts in the
Corpus Christi, Cambridge, and Cotton libraries.

---

[1] 'Merici Casauboni Is. F. De Quatuor Linguis Commentationis, Pars
prior: quæ De Lingua Hebraica: et De Lingua Saxonica. Londini, Typis
J. Flesher, 1650.'

[2] Cf. Horne Tooke, *Diversions of Purley,* and *Letter to Dr. Dunning,* for
opinions on this Greek derivation of Old English.

[3] Kennett, *Life of Somner.*

These were collated with other copies by Ralph Jennings, his amanuensis.

To adorn the work, Sir Roger Twysden was to acquaint the Reader with the occasion of the book.[1] . . . Mr. Selden was in a large preface to give account of the ten Historians, and their writings. And Mr. Jennings to subjoyn the various selections. But still the Editors were sensible that to complete the glory of the work, there wanted a Glossary, or explecation of the more obscure and obsolete words. . . . For this province they knew of none so well qualified as Mr. Somner: to him they committed the office and he discharg'd it with infinite integrity and honour. So that when in 1652 this best collection of Historians came forth under the title *Historiæ Anglicanæ Scriptores X*, the appendix was Mr. Somner's labour.[2]

Another volume of similar character was intended, but the deaths of Selden and Ussher within a few years dissolved the association of the editors. Dr. Fell purchased a lot of material for other volumes, and under his encouragement some of it was printed.

Through his connection with the glossary to *Historiæ Anglicanæ Scriptores X*, Somner gained reputation as an antiquarian scholar to such an extent that 'no Monuments of Antiquity could be farther publisht without his advise and helping hand'. Among other things, he undertook the turning of the Old English originals and English transcripts from Leland's *Itinerary* into 'plain and proper Latin: a necessary and useful ornament to those admirable volumes'.[3]

---

[1] Twysden explained that some words in the glossary were not to be found in the texts, but were inserted as helpful in understanding such other histories as might be unannotated.

[2] Kennett, *Life of Somner.*

[3] Somner translated Old English into Latin, although he strongly objected to the Latin translation of Lambarde's *Archaionomia*, and designed to translate the laws into English, 'that such Gentlemen who understood only their mother tongue might not be ignorant of these fundamental constitutions'. These Somner never printed. Cf. Kennett, *Life of Somner.*

By the middle of the seventeenth century, Old English scholarship had reached the stage where men began to realize their inability to go on without a carefully prepared dictionary, to aid them in understanding 'obscure and dubious words'. They turned naturally to Somner to supply the want. 'When', says Casaubon, 'Mr. Somner by several essays on the Saxon tongue, had sufficiently proved himself a master of it, I ceased not then to importune him that he would think of compiling a Saxon Dictionary, by which work, I did assure him, he would best merit of that language and would receive infinite thanks from all that were studious in it'.[1]   White Kennett complains bitterly of such a book being brought up on common charity, and not paying, by its sales, for its printing.   Yet Somner was unusually fortunate in his patrons and helpers. Sir Simonds D'Ewes furnished him with deeds and charters; Spelman gave him the Cambridge lecture; Junius, besides furnishing a transcript of Ælfric's Grammar, probably helped in the actual compilation, as he was much in Oxford in 1658-9.   Sir Thomas Cotton gave him access to his library, lent him glosses, and entertained him for months in his own house while the dictionary was in preparation, besides contributing to its publication.   Twysden also contributed to the expenses, as did Dugdale in return for Somner's help on the *Monasticon* (1655-61) and the Spelman *Archæologus*.

As a basis for his dictionary, Somner made use of the following:

(a) The Latin-Saxon Grammar of Ælfric, transcribed by Junius from the library of Peter Paul Rubens.   This, he says, was in rather barbarous Latin.

[1] Casaubon, *De Quatuor Linguis*, p. 142.

(b) Two manuscript dictionaries of unknown authors in the Cotton library.[1]

(c) Notes for a dictionary, unfinished, by Wheloc, compiled from *Bede*, the *Anglo-Saxon Chronicle*, the *Homilies of Ælfric*, and the *Saxon Laws*.

(d) Alfred's *Orosius*.

(e) A transcript of the *Textus Roffensis;* among printed books, Lambarde's *Archaionomia*, L'Isle's *Saxon Treatise*, Wheloc's *Bede* and *Anglo-Saxon Chronicle*, Spelman's *Archæologus*, and Verstegan's *Restitution of Decayed Intelligence*.

He also inspected the collections of Hatton, Selden, Ashmole, D'Ewes, and Arundel. Two other glosses came to him: that of Joscelyn and Parker,[2] transcribed by D'Ewes, and a transcript by Junius of Nowell's *Vocabularium Saxonicum*.[3] This latter reached Somner when most of the work was done, and so was of little use to him. It may be interesting to compare the list used by Somner with that written on the fly-leaf of Nowell's manuscript vocabulary: 'For the degrees of the declinatiō of the old Inglishe or Saxō tongue, reade,

1. The Lawes before the Conquest.

2. The Saxō chrō. of Peterborough, after the Conquest.

3. The Saxō writte of H. 3 to Oxfordshire, in ye little booke of old lawes, fo.

4. The pater n're and crede of Rob. Grosted, in the booke of Patrices purgatorie &c.

5. The rythme of Jacob in the booke called flos florū.

6. The Chronicles called Brute, Gower, Chaucer &c. By the wᶜʰ and suche like it may appeare how,

---

[1] One of these is described as a thick octavo, the other as a folio. Another Latin-'Saxon' gloss of Ælfric, written as a comment on his grammar, was in the Cotton library, and also in St. John's, Oxford. Somner did not seem to know of these.

[2] Cf. Bodl. MS. 33.

[3] MS. Seld. Arch B.; and Junius, MS. 26.

and by what steps our language is fallen frō the old Inglishe, and drawen nearer to the Frenche. This may well be lightened by shorte examples taken frō theis bookes, and its meete to be discovered when this Dictionarie shal be emprinted. W. Lambarde, 1570'.[1]

The printing of Somner's *Dictionarium Saxonico-Latino-Anglicum*[2] was the occasion of the first use of the Oxford Anglo-Saxon types.[3] The impression was made in April, 1659. The volume contains a dedication to 'Saxon' students; a dedicatory letter to Roger Spelman; a preface to the reader, in which the author reviews what had been done in Old English scholarship; a brief outline of Old English syntax; a collection of poems, laudatory of his work; and the vocabulary, in Old English, Latin, and English, followed by Ælfric's grammar and glossary. Although published in the days of anarchy and confusion, the dictionary had a fair reception from scholars, but 'this first public essay on the construction of the Saxon tongue is not so full and absolute but it is capable of additions and improvement'. Somner himself was desirous of a new edition,[4] which he did not live to accomplish.

---

[1] MS. Seld. Arch B.

[2] 'Dictionarium Saxonico-Latino-Anglicum, voces, phrasesque præcipuas Anglo-Saxonicas; e libris, sive manuscriptis, sive typis excusis, aliisque monumentis tum publicis tum privatis, magna diligentia collectas; cum Latina et Anglica vocum interpretatione complectens. Adjectis interdum exemplis, vocum etymologiis, & cum cognatis linguis collationibus, plurimisque in gratiam linguæ Anglosaxonicæ studiosorum observationibus. Opera & studio Guliel. Somneri Cantuariensis. Accesserunt Ælfrici abbatis Grammatica, Latino-Saxonica, cum Glossario suo ejusdem generis. . . . Oxonii, excudebat Guliel. Hall.' 1659, folio.

[3] Cf. Appendix III, p. 165.

[4] 'I return my thanks for these papers of Mr. Davenport, which you were pleased to impart to me. I have more than once perused them, and am so well pleased and instructed by them, that I shall improve them to a good degree: in point of correction to some, enlargement and illustration

Books such as this were mostly printed by private subscriptions, or funds obtained for the purpose. The author's return consisted in the more or less empty plaudits of his fellow-scholars and personal admirers. Part of a poem, laudatory of Somner, and printed in his dictionary, illustrates the general attitude toward such productions in the middle of the 17th century:

> Thy trade is out of fashion, friend,
> Loe, 'gainst Antiquities we now contend,
> Our quarrel is against the former age
> Gainst our dead Fathers we dire warres do wage.
> Haddst thou some Bible Dictionary made,
> A Concordance, or dealt in such like trade,
> Haddst thou some Gospel truth, some commonplace
> Presented to this fighting-preaching race
> Or to our sword Divines assistance lent,
> By Paraphrase, Expounding or Comment:
> Thou mightst have (haply) found more Readers.
> —John de Bosco.

After the dictionary, Somner published one other book connected with the study of Old English. His *History of Gavelkind* had been practically completed and officially approved by Ussher in 1647, but, owing to the turbulence of the times, and perhaps because he was bending all his energies to the completion of his dictionary, his *Gavelkind*[1] did not appear until 1660. In this work, Somner goes into great detail as to the mean-

in other parts of my Lexicon, not without acknowledgement of my author.' —Letter of Somner to Casaubon. Davenport was editor of Dugdale's *Monasticon*.

Junius made corrections and additions to a copy of Somner's Dictionary, now in the Bodleian.

Sweet characterizes Somner's dictionary as a mere glossary without references.—Cf. *King Alfred's Gregory's Pastoral*, edited for the Early English Text Society, 1871.

[1] 'A Treatise of Gavelkind, Both Name and Thing. Shewing the true Etymologie and Derivation of the one, and the Nature, Antiquity and Original of the Other.' London, 1660. New edition, White Kennett, 1726.

5

ing of the term, its origin, and the history of its function
in land-tenure in Kent. In the text are scattered illustrative passages from the ecclesiastical archives of
Canterbury, from the *Textus Roffensis*, Bede, and Lambarde's *Archaionomia*. A considerable appendix consists of Old English charters of St. Augustine's Abbey,
Canterbury, and Canterbury Cathedral. These he ac-
companies with an interlinear English translation. Some
idea of Somner's industry in his 'Saxon' studies is to
be gained by enumerating his papers preserved in Canterbury[1]: large extracts out of the chronicle of William
Thorn, from the Canterbury and Rochester Cathedral
registers, and from 'Saxon' annals; a transcript of a
large theological treatise; two volumes of material for
his dictionary; two volumes of miscellaneous Old English transcripts; copious emendations of Lambarde's
Archaionomia, Spelman's *Concilia* (which he collated
with the manuscript copy); marginal notes upon Silas
Taylor's *Gavelkind*, Selden's *Eadmer*, Spelman's *Psalterium*, Foxe's edition of the Gospels, L'Isle's *Saxon
Treatise*, and Casaubon's *De Quatuor Linguis;* a volume
of comments on Spelman's *Archæologus;* Wat's glossary
to Matthew Paris, etc.[2]

    John Selden (1584-1654) was a central figure among
seventeenth-century scholars; he was a skillful lawyer,
and, as Wood says, 'a prodigy of learning in things
uncommon'. After his Oxford days he spent most of
his time in London, in close association with such men
as Sir Robert Cotton, to whose library he possessed a
key. D'Ewes, in his *Autobiography*, says, rather primly,
that with Cotton and Selden he held 'good outward
correspondence, . . . but both of them being more
learned than pious, I never sought after or ever at-

----

[1] Many of his manuscripts, including his memoirs, were burned.

[2] Cf. Kennett, *Life of Somner*.

tained unto any great entireness with them'.[1] Selden
bore a reputation for arrogance among his contemporaries; it would seem that he was not personally
helpful to many of his fellow-antiquaries, and, in spite
of his reputation for vast learning, his scholarship did
not go unchallenged even in so uncritical an age.[2]

His relation to Old English scholarship illustrates
its place in the general scholarship of the century. In
Selden we have a man who never published an Old
English manuscript, whose reputation as a scholar was
made in other fields—as a Latinist, pre-eminently—yet
who gave more prominence to the historical uses of
Old English records than any man between Lambarde
and Dugdale. Chronologically his career is interesting,
when compared with landmarks in Old English scholarship. His *Eadmer* appeared the same year as L'Isle's
Saxon Treatise; he became keeper of the Tower Rolls
the year that Wheloc published Bede's *Ecclesiastical
History* and the *Anglo-Saxon Chronicle,* and he died
five years before the issue of Somner's *Dictionarium.*
When we consider Selden's work by itself, we find that
the *Janus Anglorum,* 1610, shows evidence of considerable knowledge of Old English laws, although
there are but few citations from such sources.[3] His
attitude on the origin of English law is interestingly
set forth in the preface: 'To refer the original of our
English Laws to that Conquest, is a huge mistake; for
as much as they are of a far more ancient Date. For
it is a remark amongst Statesmen, that new acquired
Empires do run some hazard by attempting to make

[1] D'Ewes, *Autobiography,* p. 256.

[2] Hickes, in the preface to his grammar, states that only Joscelyn, Junius,
Marshall and Somner published their 'Saxon' accurately; he mentions
Selden as one of the inaccurate editors. Selden's works were republished
by Wilkins, 1726, as *Johannis Seldeni Jurisconsulti Opera Omnia.*

[3] There are only a few scattered Old English words cited.

new Laws; and the Normans did warily provide against
this danger, by bestowing upon the yielding conquered
Nation the requital of their ancient Law'.[1] In *Titles
of Honour*, 1630, he quotes five times as many passages
of Old English as in the first edition,[2] 1614. This seems
to indicate the general increase of interest in Old English records after L'Isle's publication in 1623. Nor
must we overlook the fact that his *History of Tithes*
quotes rather freely from Old English sources, at a
time when there appeared to be no interest in the study
of the language. His famous *Mare Clausum*, 1635, extended the use of Old English documentary evidence.
Heretofore it had been used to explain various prac-
tices in land-tenure,[3] but never before Selden was it
applied as a precedent in laws concerning the high seas.

Selden's interest in Old English bore one very definite result—the procuring of Anglo-Saxon types for
the learned press at Oxford. He was in correspondence
with Junius relative to such types, just before his
death.[4] Through his marriage with a former Countess
of Kent,[5] he was possessed of an ample fortune, which
enabled him to collect a remarkable library. This he
destined for Oxford; but, angered because the University would not lend him manuscripts, he willed the
collection, containing many manuscripts and printed
books relating to Old English studies, to his executors,
who finally bestowed it upon Oxford.[6]

William Dugdale (1605-1686) was an enthusiastic

---

[1] *Janus Anglorum*, 2d edition, 1683 (an English translation of the 1610
edition).

[2] Five brief extracts, 1614; twenty-five, 1630.

[3] Especially in Lambarde's works.

[4] Cf. Appendix III, p. 165. These types were purchased by the University.

[5] Widow of Henry, Earl of Kent.

[6] Cf. Appendix I, No. 9.

'Saxonist' of the mid-seventeenth century. With him we associate the name of Roger Dodsworth (1585-1654), because of his collaboration in the *Monasticon*. Dugdale had a natural taste for collecting old monastic records, and as a young man received much encouragement in his 'Saxon' studies from Sir Henry Spelman. Dodsworth, who was also Spelman's friend, had gathered many records relating to the foundations of monasteries in the north of England.[1] Spelman thought his collections might be expanded into a description of all the monasteries, with a history of their charters. He persuaded Dugdale to join in the enterprise, offering his own transcripts from Norfolk and Suffolk. He also recommended Dugdale to the Earl of Arundel and to Sir Christopher Hatton,[2] through whose influence Dugdale was admitted to the Heralds' College, where he rose to great prominence, and was knighted in 1677. Meanwhile he went on with his compilation, depositing his transcripts of Westminster Abbey records in Sir Christopher Hatton's library. Having attended King Charles to Oxford, he employed his long stay in transcribing charters and other records in the Bodleian and the college libraries. Other records he gathered from the Cotton library, from the Tower records, and from the papers of Duchesne, whom he visited at Paris. The results of the labors of Dodsworth and Dugdale appeared as the *Monasticon Anglicanum*, in three parts, 1655-1673.[3] So highly was this compilation valued that, when the various charters in it were not available, the book was admitted in Westminster Court as 'circumstantial evidence'.[4] Dugdale's

---

[1] His transcripts from York were timely, as many of the originals were destroyed in the civil wars.

[2] Cf. Gibson, *Life of Spelman*, 1723.

[3] *Monasticon* 1, 1655; 2, 1661; 3, 1673 (folio).

[4] Cf. Preface to *Monasticon* abridged, 1693.

most distinctive work, the *History of St. Paul's*, contains several charters of the Anglo-Saxon kings. After the destructions wrought by civil war and the great fire of London, these collections made by Dugdale and Dodsworth[1] became doubly valuable, as preserving transcripts of manuscripts that had perished. Besides his own numerous works of an historical character, Dugdale edited Sir Henry Spelman's unfinished papers.[2]

The interest of Old English scholarship in the first half of the seventeenth century centred in glossaries and historical documents of a legal or theological character. Francis Junius (1589-1677) gave the world its first purely literary interest in Old English by the publication of Cædmon, 1655.[3] It is significant of the nature of the revival of Old English that it took eighty-nine years to produce a scholar who could sufficiently detach himself from the controversial interest in English antiquities to print a document not primarily theological or historical; and it is also significant that this greatest of Old English scholars was not English. His father was French, his mother from the Netherlands.[4] Born at Heidelberg, he passed his youth in Leyden, where his father was a divinity-professor. When about twenty he went to reside in France, coming to England in 1620. He soon became acquainted with Laud, then Bishop of St. David's, through whom, probably, he was made librarian to Thomas Howard, Earl of Arundel. During his long residence in England, his great learning and his urbane manner endeared him to English scholars. He returned

---

[1] Dodsworth left sixty volumes of transcripts.

[2] Cf. p. 49.

[3] This is the first Old English poetry printed, except a brief extract in *Historiæ Anglicanæ*, 1652.

[4] Cf. Paul, *Grundriss* 1. 2. 26-27.

to the Netherlands for a time, where he made further study of northern languages, publishing his Cædmon[1] in 1655, and the Gospels,[2] in conjunction with Marshall, in 1665. In 1674 he returned to England for the sake of the Cottonian and Bodleian libraries, and after a residence of two years at Oxford, presumably with his friend and pupil, Thomas Marshall, then Rector of Lincoln College, he went to visit his nephew, Isaac Vossius, Canon of Windsor, and there died, and was buried in St. George's Chapel. Wood says that Junius returned to Oxford especially because he wished to be buried there, and because he wished to bequeath his manuscripts to the University, and that he was so bothered by visitors while in the lodgings of Dr. Marshall that he sought retirement in Beef-hall Lane (St. Ebb's), where he continued to put his papers in order, and arrange for their reception at the Bodleian.[3]

His natural aptitude for languages, his early training in Teutonic dialects, together with a remarkable exactness in transcribing manuscripts, made him surpass any of his predecessors or contemporaries in the field of Old English scholarship. He was the first scholar to make a really scientific study of northern dialects in conjunction with Old English. He transcribed many

[1] 'Cædmonis Monachi Paraphrasis Poetica Genesios ac præcipuarum sacræ paginæ Historiarum, abhinc annos MLXX. Anglo Saxonice conscripta, et nunc primum edita a Francisco Junio F. F. Amsteliodami apud Christophorum Cunradi, typis et sumptibus editoris.' 1655. 4to.

[2] 'Quatuor D. N. Jesu Christi Euangeliorum Versiones perantiquæ duæ, Gothica scil. et Anglo-Saxonica: quarum illam ex celeberrimo Codice Argenteo nunc primum depromsit Franciscus Junius, F. F. Hanc autem ex Codicibus MSS. collatis emendatius recudi curavit Thom. Mareschallus, Anglus: cujus etiam Observationes in utramque Versionem subnectuntur. Accessit et Glossarium Gothicum; cui præmittitur Alphabetum Gothicum, Runicum, etc, opera ejusdem Francisci Junii. Dordrechti. Typis et sumptibus Juianis. Excudebant Henricus et Johannes Essæ, urbis typographi ordinarii.' 1665. 4to.

[3] Wood, *Fasti Oxonienses* 2. 337.

glossaries, and planned a dictionary as early as 1654.[1] Unfortunately, he did not live to publish such a work. His numerous transcripts from glossaries, a much annotated copy of Somner's dictionary, and the manuscript of his *Etymologicum* in the Bodleian, testify to his perseverance in dictionary-making.[2] The *Etymologicum* was not published until 1743, and then by Edward Lye, who seems to have been unequal to the task. Lye himself compiled an Old English dictionary, mostly copied from Junius' materials, but this was not published until 1772, by Owen Manning.

Cædmon was printed (with types which Junius provided for the purpose) from a manuscript originally belonging to Ussher, ten years before Milton completed *Paradise Lost*. The Gospels, prepared with the help of Marshall, brings us to the consideration of another energetic figure among Oxford 'Saxonists'. Thomas Marshall (1621-1685) was a Lincoln College man, and a great admirer of Ussher, whom he was accustomed to hear preach at All Saints' Church. It is probably through Ussher that he came to know Junius, and, about the time that Parliament convened at Oxford, he migrated to Holland, where for some time he was preacher to the company of English merchants at Rotterdam and Dort. Marshall's desire to study German for the sake of perfecting his Old English led him to spend this time abroad. Meanwhile, Junius had obtained the use of the famous *Codex Argenteus*, and was preparing an edition of the Gospels in Gothic and Old English, parallel. To this work Marshall

[1] Cf. letter to Selden, May, 1654: 'Having met here in these our parts with four MSS glossaries, &c, I begin to think myself now so well instructed with good subsidyes as that I shal be bold to try how to nd something to what Goldastus and Freherus have commented in that line.'

[2] In the Bodleian are eight volumes of Junius' manuscript lexicons, mostly of Teutonic dialects.

added copious notes, both on the Gothic and the Old English versions. To the fame he attained by this work, if we may credit Wood,[1] he owed his election as a fellow of Lincoln College in 1668. His return to Oxford greatly promoted Old English studies, and at Dr. Fell's suggestion he began collections for a grammar. A fragment of this work is noted in Wanley's Catalogue as *Grammaticalia quædam Anglo-Saxonica per D. Thomam Mareschallum, in solutis schedis scripta, et inter codd. ejus MSS. reposita.*[2] Another of his unfinished works was an edition of *Orosius;*[3] with this undertaking he progressed as far as collating a Junian transcript with the Lauderdale manuscript.[4]

Archbishops Laud and Ussher did much to establish interest in Old English. Sir Henry Spelman acknowledged encouragement from Laud in his edition of the *Concilia*. Sir John Spelman dedicated the *Psalterium* to him as a patron of the language, and preserver of its manuscripts. He was the friend and patron of both Junius and Somner. It was Ussher who urged Spelman to the founding of the Cambridge lecture in 'Saxon', and who suggested Wheloc for the office, advised him in his studies, and urged on his publications. Besides furnishing Junius with the Cædmon manuscript, he contributed to its publication, and recommended Somner to succeed Wheloc as Cambridge lecturer. The library of Laud eventually furnished Oxford with a wonderful collection of Old English manuscripts, both originals and transcripts.

The patronage of these men was followed by that of Dr. John Fell, whose close personal association with

---

[1] *Athenæ Oxonienses* 4. 170-171.

[2] Wanley, p. 102.

[3] Daines Barrington published *Orosius,* 1773.

[4] Nicolson, *Historical Library,* p. 42; Nichols, *Literary Anecdotes,* p. 4.

the band of 'Saxonists' gradually forming in the University led him to provide the Oxford learned press with new fonts of Anglo-Saxon types about 1672.[1] Undoubtedly the patronage of Laud, Ussher, and Fell, together with the publication of Somner's dictionary at the University press, turned the tide of Old English scholarship toward Oxford. The addition of Selden's and of Junius' wonderful collections, and of the Junian Anglo-Saxon types, did much to sustain this interest; but probably the presence of Junius and of Marshall in their midst aroused more enthusiasm than all the collections belonging to the University. When we consider that the great grammarian of the northern languages, George Hickes, was the pupil of Marshall, the latter becomes a very important person in the progress of Old English scholarship.

In the latter part of the seventeenth century there sprang up what Rowe Mores called a 'profluvium of Saxonists'[2] at Oxford. This coterie, mostly Queen's and University College men, furnish the most unique chapter in the history of Old English scholarship. Beginning with Marshall and Junius, and extending down to Thomas Hearne, they absorbed every branch of Old English learning—theological, historical, antiquarian, and linguistic. It was part of their definite plan to publish manuscripts that had never been printed, to make catalogues of existing collections, and to act as instructors in the language. Their varied activities won for them the title of 'Saxonists', a name which, although occasionally applied to other Old English scholars, is the peculiar property of these men. Hickes and Thwaites were the ruling spirits in this band of scholars, which included Nicolson, Gibson,

---

[1] Cf. Appendix III.

[2] Rowe Mores, *English Typographical Founders.*

Benson, Christopher Rawlinson, the Elstobs, Wanley, Charlett, Hudson, and Tanner.

George Hickes (1642-1715), a Yorkshire man, was first a servitor at St. John's College, Oxford, 1659, then of Magdalen, and then Fellow of Lincoln, 1664. Here he met Marshall, and became his pupil in 'Saxon'. As a nonjuror, he was deprived of ecclesiastical preferment in 1690. Throughout his career he engaged in a pamphlet-war, which made him many enemies. Swift saw fit to attack his pet hobby, the study of northern languages, so that this philologist and divine became a target in the Swift-Temple-Wotton controversy.[1] In spite of partisan feeling, Hickes found time to prepare, and patrons to further, the first Old English grammar, 1689.[2] This gave a great impetus to the study of the language and to the publication of manuscripts.

William Nicolson (1655-1727) entered Queen's College in 1670, and became Fellow in 1679. The year before, he had spent some time at Leipzig studying German. The trip was made at the expense of Sir Joseph Williamson, and shortly after Nicolson's return to Oxford we get the first hint of a 'Saxon' class (which it is said Sir Joseph instituted, with Nicolson as lecturer), held every Wednesday in term-time.[3] Nicolson left Oxford for a stall at Carlisle, 1682,[4] seven years before Hickes published his shorter grammar. For a time he collaborated with Gibson on an edition of the *Anglo-Saxon Chronicle*, a work which it appears Junius had suggested to him, but published nothing himself from Old English manuscripts. He was, however, in regular correspondence with the 'Saxonists', and helped

---

[1] Cf. Elizabeth Elstob's defense of Hickes in the preface to her *Rudiments of Grammar* (Appendix II), and Wotton, *Remarks on the Tale of a Tub.*

[2] Cf. chap. III.

[3] Cf. Magrath, *The Flemings at Oxford* 1. 302.

[4] Bishop of Carlisle, 1702.

raise funds for publishing their works.[1] His *Historical Library*, 1692-96, is invaluable for the history of Old English scholarship.[2]

Edmund Gibson (1668-1748) entered Queen's in 1686. He became M. A. in 1694, and held a fellowship which he resigned in 1701. For a time he was librarian to Archbishop Tenison at Lambeth, passing through various ecclesiastical preferments until he became Bishop of Lincoln in 1715, and was transferred to London in 1723. While still at Oxford, he undertook an edition of the *Anglo-Saxon Chronicle*,[3] continuing the work that Nicolson had begun. It is presumed that Nicolson's knowledge of German would have greatly aided this edition, but his removal to the bishopric of Derry prevented his active coöperation, and the whole credit of the work went to Gibson, who was only twenty-four years old when it appeared in 1692. In his preface, Gibson states that Gerard Langbaine, Provost of Queen's 1646-58, had undertaken an edition, but was forestalled by Wheloc, whose work was full of defects. The Queen's men were anxious to put out an improved edition. Besides correcting the Wheloc text, Gibson made a new and more literal Latin translation, printed parallel with the Old English. The difficulties he encountered in this task were greatly lessened by the grammar of Hickes. This edition, then, is the first Old English text prepared with the help of a grammar

---

[1] Cf. Appendix I, Nos. 11, 13, 16, 17, 18, 24.

[2] His letters, edited by John Nichols in 1809, also furnish valuable information on this period.

[3] 'Chronicon Saxonicum, seu Annales rerum in Anglia praecipue gestarum, a Christo nato ad annum usque MCLIV deducti, ac jam demum Latinitate donati. Cum Indice rerum chronologico. Accedunt regulæ ad investigandas nominum locorum origines. Et nominum locorum ac virorum in Chronico memoratorum explicatio. Opera et studio Edmundi Gibson, A. B. e Collegio Reginæ Oxoniæ, e Theatro Sheldoniano.' 1692.

and dictionary.[1] Gibson edited one other work relating to Old English studies before he left Oxford permanently. This was a collection of Sir Henry Spelman's papers, which he published under the title *Reliquiæ Spelmannianæ*, 1698. These were mostly essays relating to laws and antiquities, the bulk of them in English, with a few Latin passages. To this Gibson prefixed a life of Spelman, which gives some interesting information as to the state of 'Saxon' learning in the seventeenth century.

Twenty years before, Obadiah Walker, Master of University College, and Christopher Ware, had published Sir John Spelman's life of King Alfred,[2] which he had compiled at Oxford during his attendance upon the king.[3] Ware translated the manuscript into Latin, and Walker added a considerable appendix, which Hearne says passed as Spelman's additions, but was not in the original.[4] Obadiah Walker was an ardent Roman Catholic, and, naturally, since critical sense in the editing of manuscripts was uncommon in his day, he did not hesitate to add anything he saw fit that would favor Roman Catholicism; in consequence, the attention of Parliament was called to the fact that Oxford was printing works that might be construed as favoring that religion.[5] The episode of Walker's edi-

[1] No Old English text had appeared in England since Somner's dictionary was printed; the only other important text between Somner and Gibson was the Dort Gospels of Junius, 1665.

[2] 'Ælfredi Magni Anglorum Regis invictissimi Vita tribus libris comprehensa a clarissimo Dⁿᵒ Johanne Spelman Henrici F. primum Anglice conscripta, dein Latine reddita, et annotationibus illustrata ab Ælfredi in Collegio Magnæ Aulæ Universitatis Oxoniensis Alumnis. Oxonii, e Theatro Sheldoniano.' 1678. fol.

[3] Cf. p. 50.

[4] Hearne, *The Life of Ælfred the Great*, 1709. These additions included Alfred's Old English version of the Preface to Gregory's *Pastoral Care*, and the *Voyages of Ohthere and Wulstan*.

[5] Cf. Wood, *Athenæ Oxonienses* 4. 439.

tion of Spelman's *Alfred* is an instance of the continued perversion of materials for controversial purposes which attached to the first use of English antiquities a hundred years earlier.

Edward Thwaites (1677-1711) entered Queen's the same year that Hickes published his grammar, and at once became a leader among the 'Saxonists'. In 1698 he was elected dean of his college, and the same year we get another definite mention of actual instruction given to a class in Old English. In a letter to Humphrey Wanley, March 24, 169⅝, he says: 'We want Saxon Lexicons. I have fifteen young students in that language, and but one Somner for them all'. This deficiency he tried to remedy by an abridgment of Somner, which eventually appeared as the work of Thomas Benson in 1701. Among the Rawlinson manuscripts[1] is a fragment of four printed leaves, entitled, *Thesaurus Linguæ Anglo-Saxonicæ Dictionario Gul. Somneri, quod numerum vocum, auctior. Cura Thomæ Benson, e Collegio Reginæ. Oxoniæ e Theatro Sheldoniano. An. 1690.* To this is added four pages in the writing of Thwaites—a Latin-Saxon specimen of Gregory's *Pastoral Care* which he designed to publish. It seems probable that the abridgment of Somner was more the work of Thwaites than of Benson. When Benson's abridgment finally appeared, the title was somewhat altered.[2] From an entry in Hearne's diary, it would seem that this lexicon was the joint product of Thwaites, Todhunter, Benson, and several unknown students of Queen's.[3] In this abridgment are

[1] MS. Rawl. D. 377, fol. 80.

[2] 'Vocabularium Anglo-Saxonicum, Lexico Gul. Somneri magna parte auctius Opera Thomæ Benson, Art. Bac. e Collegio Reginæ.' 1701.

[3] Humphrey Wanley made an abridgment, probably for his own use. 1692, MS. Harl. 3317.

some additions to Somner taken from the Junian manuscript vocabularies in the Bodleian.[1]

Thwaites' principal publication was the *Heptateuchus*,[2] 1698. He had long contemplated editing the Pentateuch, as is evident from various letters regarding it;[3] specimens were circulated in 1697. Nicolson, particularly, did all in his power to further the publication, but regretted that it was not more complete, and that it lacked a Latin translation. In a letter to Thwaites, 1698, he says: 'I wish the Pentateuch were more entire. . . . I wish you had given us the Vulgar Latin with it. It looks indeed more masterly and more becoming an University edition, to have a book sent abroad that supposes it shall meet with plenty of readers that shall understand it as readily as the publisher does; but perhaps it would sell as well if it had brought along with it a help towards its interpretation. The world is not as well stocked with men skilled in our Saxon language and antiquities as we may hope to see it.'[4] Thwaites followed the dictates of affection rather than of prudence by inscribing his work to Hickes. The political situation was such that the heads of colleges feared that such a dedication would be offensive at court. In the dedication and preface Thwaites says that the five books of Moses, with Joshua and Judges, are from Ælfric's manuscript in the Bodleian; the book of Job from an Ælfric manuscript, to which L'Isle had added a version in the Cotton library; Nicodemus was transcribed by Junius from the

[1] Cf. Appendix I, No. 24.

[2] 'Heptateuchus, Liber Job, et Evangelium Nicodemi; Anglo-Saxonice. Historiæ Judith fragmentum; Dano-Saxonice. Edidit nunc prĭmum ex MSS. codicibus Edwardes Thwaites, e Collegio Reginæ. Oxoniæ e Theatro Sheldoniano.' 1698. 8°.

[3] Cf. Appendix I, Nos. 8, 11, 17.

[4] Nicolson, *Correspondence*, Vol. 1, No. 46.

Benet College, Cambridge, manuscript, to which he
added variants. Though much contained in the volume
was the work of Junius, or results of his work, and
fittingly printed with his types, Thwaites dedicated it
to Hickes as 'literaturæ hujus omnis instauratori
maximo'. Gibson had warned Thwaites to exclude any
passages favorable to Popery,[1] and Nicolson was
dubious about printing Nicodemus at such a time.[2]
The addition of Judith[3] might likewise have been open
to criticism, but probably the polemic factions did not
consider poetry as serious testimony on one side or
the other.

Christopher Rawlinson (1677-1733), one of the
Queen's 'Saxonists', brought out Boethius' *Consola-
tiones*,[4] also in 1698. This is printed from the Junian
manuscript, which had additions from the Cottonian
version,[5] later destroyed. There was no attempt at
translation, either into Latin or English. The preface
is probably by Thwaites, so that Rawlinson was practically little more than an amanuensis for the edition,
which was limited to two hundred and fifty copies.
Many of these were distributed as gifts, and, according
to Nicolson, they were of great help to Hickes in getting subscribers to his *Thesaurus*.[6] The practice of
limited editions seems to have grown upon Oxford

[1] Appendix I, No. 8.

[2] Nichols, *Literary Anecdotes* 4. 145.

[3] The only other specimen of Old English poetry printed in England
was in Twysden's *Historiæ Anglicanæ*, 1652.

[4] 'An Manl. Sever. Boethi Consolationis Philosophiæ libri V. Anglo-
Saxonice redditi ab Alfredo Inclyto Anglo-Saxonum Rege. Ad apographum
Junianum expressos edidit Christophorus Rawlinson, a Collegio Reginæ,
Oxoniæ, e Theatro Sheldoniano. 1698. 8°. (Sumptibus editoris, typis
Junianis).'

[5] Cott. Otho A. VI.

[6] Thoresby, *Correspondence*, Vol. 1.

Saxonists', as witness Hickes' *Thesaurus*, and Hearne's numerous works.[1]

There are a number of works of lesser importance that deserve passing mention among seventeenth-century Old English studies. In 1663, Silas Taylor published his *Gavelkind*, containing a meagre account of the gradual extinction of the 'Saxon' language, and including a few quotations from the *Anglo-Saxon Chronicle*. Wood complains of the way Taylor garbled the extracts he made from Hereford and Worcester.[2] His transcripts from the Hereford *Doomsday Book* are in the Harleian collection.

In 1670, Sheringham published *De Anglorum Gentis Origine*, which was highly praised in its day as a scholarly investigation of the origin of the races which had peopled the British Isles. Aylett Sammes is accused of copying Sheringham's theories wholesale in his own *Antiquities of Ancient Britain*, 1676. In this latter book are a few 'Saxon' specimens, from the *Textus Roffensis* and the *Laws of Ine*. Sammes is, rather rudely, called an 'impertinent pedant', who, according to Wood, never saw the books from which he quoted.[3] He asserts that the Saxons are of 'Getish' extraction.

More interesting than these compilations is a group of essays of a philological character. The relation of English to the languages of the world had by this time been borne in upon the scholars in various fields. In 1683 was published Sir Thomas Browne's *Certain Miscellany Tracts*, among which is an essay 'of Languages, and particularly of the Saxon Tongue'. The examples which he gives as Old English are more

---

[1] Cf. Appendix I, No. 32.

[2] *Athenæ Oxonienses* 3. 1176.

[3] Cf. Gough, *Topographical Antiquities* 2. 369.

properly Middle English, but the early scholars did not recognize the difference between these successive stages of the language.

In 1688, William Cave published an interesting volume in Latin—a kind of index of old writers.[1] The works are arranged in tabular form, including editions and manuscripts then remaining unedited.

One philological treatise, frankly based on Skinner's *Etymologicon Anglicanum*,[2] deserves a more extended notice, because of the emphasis it places on Modern English as a medium of interpreting the earlier stages of the language. This book is the *Gazophylacium Anglicanum*,[3] by an anonymous writer, published in 1689. It is a curious coincidence that this book appeared in the same year as the Old English grammar of Hickes. The author explains his methods and his views in the preface. He says:

> Observe that all along, through the Book, that word is set next the English, from which I have judged it most likely to be derived, and the synonymous Words of other European Languages follow. . . . Note that very many of the Words being of a British or Saxon Original, here have their explanation set down. . . . I have forbore, as much as possible, the setting down such as are purely of a Latin Original, . . . it having been the only Fault of those that have hitherto writ upon this Subject, to be both voluminous, high-pric'd, and in Latin, so that many Well-wishers to

[1] *Scriptorum Ecclesiasticorum Historia Literaria a Christo nato usque ad Sæculum XIV, facile methodo digesto.* 1688, 2 vols., fol.

[2] Completed and published by Thomas Henshaw, 1671.

[3] 'Gazophylacium Anglicanum: containing the Derivation of English words, proper and common; each in an Alphabet distinct: Proving the Dutch and Saxon to be prime Fountains. And likewise giving the Similar Words in most European Languages, whereby any of them may be indifferently well Learned and Understood, Fitted to the Capacity of the English Reader, that may be curious to know the Original of his Mother-tongue.' London, 1689.

their Mother Tongue could neither reach the Value nor Knowledge thereof; all which I hope I have remedied by doing this in English, and in a small Volume, fitted to a small Price.

Among historical works were three that came out near the close of the century. They are the *Historia Dogmatica* of Ussher, edited by Henry Wharton, 1690; *Anglia Sacra*, by Wharton, 1691; and *Historia Britannica*, by Thomas Gale, 1691. Of these, the *Historia Dogmatica* exhibits copious specimens of Old English, and contains many references on the part of the editor to the works of Lambarde, L'Isle, and Hickes, and to the manuscript collections of Cambridge and Oxford. Thomas Gale was probably not more than a passing student of Old English, but he was in close touch with the 'Saxonists' at Oxford, where his *Historia* was published, and he is frequently spoken of as well versed in the early history of the country. Whether through his own studies or at second-hand, he made considerable use of Old English documents.

One of the noticeable tendencies of the later seventeenth century was the inclination to edit not only Old English manuscripts, but the posthumous papers of earlier scholars in this field. In addition to Wharton's Ussher, Gibson's *Reliquiæ Spelmannianæ*, Walker's Spelman's *Ælfredi Magni Vita*, which have already been mentioned, there was an edition of Sir Henry Spelman's *Discourses of Law Terms*, 1684, and Somner's *Roman Ports and Forts*, edited by James Brome, 1693, with a biography of Somner by White Kennett.

In general, the Old English scholarship of the seventeenth century expended itself on the compilation of dictionaries and grammars, and on the extension of the historical and legal uses of Old English documents. In addition to these, there were made accessible in print the Psalms, Bede, the Anglo-Saxon Chronicle, the

Heptateuch, and Boethius. By the end of the century, too, most of the great collections of Old English manuscripts had found their places much as they are to-day,[1] and Old English had become a university study, instead of the pastime of antiquaries. The seventeenth century marks greater achievements in the history of Old English scholarship in England than does the succeeding century.

[1] Cf. Appendix IV.

CHAPTER III

The Contributions to Old English Scholarship in the Eighteenth Century

We might reasonably expect the eighteenth century greatly to develop Old English scholarship. Such uncertainty in civil and ecclesiastical affairs existed in England from the Reformation to near the close of the seventeenth century that, at times, activity in Old English research was inexpedient, perhaps dangerous. The students of the language had been ninety-three years without a dictionary, one hundred and thirty-two years without a grammar, and one hundred and thirty-nine years without a general catalogue of existing manuscripts. All these wants were supplied in the opening years of the eighteenth century. With such equipment, it seems surprising that so little advance was made in the study of Old English. The difficulty lies in the fact that Latin was persistently used as a medium of interpretation. At the very outset of the Old English revival, Parker and Foxe used English translations, not because they understood the fitness of such a method, but for th sake of a controversial point. As soon, however, as Old English was taken up by general scholars, Latin was employed for translations and explications. This unhappy circumstance may be traced to two causes, aside from the prevailing habit of Latinizing everything. First, the analogy between Old English and Latin grammar was unquestioned, because of the Latin grammar of Ælfric, with its paradigms in the vernacular (Old English). The other difficulty lay in the manuscripts, many of which were Latin and Old English interlinear, the Old English being intended for those who could not read Latin. Of course we must recognize the fact that the Latin furnished a key to an entirely obsolete language, but the early philologists took for granted the relation of the 'Saxon' to classic models, and constructed their syntax accordingly. Although they vaguely recognized a similarity between Old English and the Teutonic dialects, it did not occur to them that these, too, were not traceable to classical sources.

Hickes did much to perpetuate the mistake, with his *Institutiones Grammaticæ*,[1] begun under the supervision of Marshall, and published in 1689. As far as the grammatical portions are concerned, there is little difference between this edition and the ponderous *Thesaurus* of 1705, and we may consider them together. Shortly after he was deprived of his ecclesiastical rights[2] in 1690, his friends began to urge Hickes to continue his studies in the northern dialects, as a means of taking his mind off his troubles. The views which he expressed to Charlett in a letter dated 1694 are essentially the same as the theory he sought to work out in his grammars. He says, in part:

There are four old original languages, the Greek, the Slavonic, the Gothic, and the Celtic or ancient British, and he that understands them all, as an ingenious Welshman who hath learned Greek may easily do, will be able to illustrate the harmony of languages ancient and modern, Latin also comprehended, because it is little else but Greek. . . . The harmony of lan-

[1] 'Institutiones Grammaticæ Anglo-Saxonicæ, et Moeso-Gothicæ. Auctore Georgio Hickesio Ecclesiæ Anglicanæ Presbytero, etc. Oxoniæ, e Theatro Sheldoniano,' 1689. 4°. The grammar consists of 18 chapters, 114 pages. To this is added 'Grammatica Islandica Rudolphi Jonæ, Catalogus Librorum Septentrionalium, accedit Edvardi Bernardi Etymologicon Britannicum.'

[2] As Dean of Worcester.

guages, and the light they give to antiquity, is very
pleasant, but yet a man after all will meet with disap-
pointments in these, as well as other studies; as for
example, I thought after having learned the old Northern languages, I should have understood in part the
Lapland language, as well as the Swedish, but there is
not any likeness or communication between them as
Scheffer[1] told me before, but I could not believe it before I tried, and whether that have any affinity with
the Sclavonian, I cannot say. I believe not, and therefore it may well pass for the language of witches. I
suppose the Veneti or Finlanders speak somewhat like
them. I was also pleased with the affinity our own
language had with the ancient Northern languages, in
all but French and Latin words, and yet there are
four common words in it, neither originally French
nor Latin, which are not to be derived from them, viz.,
lad, lass, boy, girl, the last of which Mr. Junius, much
below his great understanding, will needs like a pedant,
more than a wise Etymologist, derive from garrula,
so unwilling sometimes are the greatest men to be
baffled in their profession, and he certainly was a very
great man, and a very modest man. . . . The
American writers assure us that there are new independent languages almost behind every mountain in
America, and therefore it is not so strange that there
is one or two in Europe which have no relation to the
rest.[2]

In the *Thesaurus*, Hickes outlines the following
plan for the study of northern languages. Read the
'Saxon' grammar, chapters 1-17 (dealing with the
parts of speech)[3]; then the Old English Gospels of Marshall; the *Psalterium* of John Spelman; the *Heptateuchus* of Thwaites; Ælfric's *Homily*, and the *Saxon
Treatise* of L'Isle; Alfred's *Bede*, edited by Wheloc;

[1] John Scheffer (1621-1679), German antiquary, and Professor at the
University of Upsala.

[2] Cf. Bliss, *Letters from the Bodleian*, 1813, No. 30.

[3] The remainder of the enlarged grammar was not intended for be-
ginners.

Boethius, edited by Rawlinson; Spelman's *Concilia,* and Lambarde's *Archaionomia.* From these the student may pass to the Moeso-Gothic grammar, after which he can read the fragments of the Gothic Gospels, edited by Junius. The Icelandic comes next, or Scando-Gothic, as he calls it, which helps the student to interpret the Gothic of the Middle Ages. This may be followed by the Icelandic Bible, and extracts from Danish and Swedish histories. After the *Heimskringla,* published by Peringskiöld,[1] he advises Resenius' *Islandic Edda,*[2] which embraces all northern mythology. Such a course of reading, he assures us, will render any student proficient in all northern dialects.

The *Thesaurus*[3] is in two parts, the first consisting of the three grammars, (a) Old English and Mœso-Gothic, (b) Franco-Theotisc, (c) Icelandic; with a dissertation on Anglo-Saxon coins, by Sir Andrew Fountaine. The second part consists of Wanley's catalogue of Old English manuscripts and printed books.[4] This catalogue, which Thwaites turned into Latin, is the only part of the huge work that has real value for the modern student; yet, because the views of Hickes embody the scholarly ideal of Old English philology until well into the nineteenth century, they are worth

---

[1] John Peringskiöld (1654-1720), Swedish historian, published *Heims-kringla,* Stockholm, 1697.

[2] *Islandic Edda,* published 1665, by Pader Resen (1625-1688), Danish philologist.

[3] 'Antiquæ Literaturæ Septentrionalis Libri Duo, quorum Primus Georgii Hickesii, S. T. P. Linguarum Vett. Septentrionalium Thesaurum Grammatico-Criticum & Archæologicum, Ejusdem de antiquæ Literaturæ Septentrionalis Utilitate Dissertationem Epistolarem, Et Andreæ Fountaine Equitis Aurati Numismata Saxonica & Dano-Saxonica complectitur. Alter continet Humfredi Wanleii Librorum Vett. Septentrionalium, qui in Angliæ Biblioth. extant, Catalogum Historico-Criticum, nec non multorum Vett. Codd. Septentrionalium alibi extantium notitiam cum totius operis sex Indicibus. Oxoniæ, E Theatro Sheldoniano.' 1705, folio.

[4] The grammars were printed in 1703; the remainder in 1705.

reviewing. He divides Old English into three periods. The first of these extends to the Danish invasion, and he calls it British-Saxon; in this period he would put only Cædmon, Bede, and perhaps the Gospels in the Cotton library. The second period extends to the Norman Conquest; this he calls Dani-Saxon; he recognizes that this has degenerated from the pure 'Saxon' of Alfred, Ælfric, Wulfstan, and others, and notes that this stage of the language furnishes both prose and poetry. The third period extends to the reign of Henry II. Of the Semi-Saxon used in the South and West of England, he declares that a corruption of the pure tongue, by ignorance and the Danish influence, has produced modern English. In poetry, he recognizes a strict observance of metre—long and short syllables— but finds the quantity of the syllables is not often known; he further recognizes that the Old English poetry lacks end-rhyme, but seems unaware of its peculiar alliterative quality.[1] One thing Hickes discovered by his study of the various dialects, and that was that many so-called Old English charters are forgeries, since they are full of Norman phraseology.

The work was ponderous and costly—wholly unfit for the ordinary student, and swollen to its unwieldiness by the copious examples of the language in all stages of development, used as illustrative material. The original plan was for a one-volume work, which seems to have been well under way in 1698, when proposals were issued.[2] In 1699 Nicolson complained that adding the tables of coins would long delay the work, for which subscribers were already becoming impatient;[3] yet it dragged on for another six years, during

---

[1] The Judith-fragment in Thwaites' *Heptateuchus* is printed as prose.

[2] Cf. Appendix I, Nos. 13 and 16.

[3] *Ibid.*, No. 18.

which time its friends and supporters were often put to shifts to prevent paid subscriptions from being withdrawn.[1]   Thwaites superintended the printing, Nicolson helped in portions of the composition, Gibson sent Hickes valuable manuscripts,[2] Elstob translated the Wulfstan homily into Latin and added notes,[3] William Hopkins[4] sent the Old English commentary on saints buried in England, and Brome compiled the six indexes.

The nature of Wanley's catalogue is such that it deserves separate mention, and with it we may consider the career of the man himself.   Humphrey Wanley (1671-1726) was early apprenticed to a limner in his native town of Coventry.   His passion for the study of manuscripts and their peculiarities soon made him famous in his locality for his ability to distinguish their ages.   William Lloyd, who was then Bishop of Coventry, persuaded his father to send him to Oxford, where he became a battler at St. Edmund's Hall.   He was not particularly happy under the direction of Dr. Mill, the Principal, and Hearne records that he attended but one lecture—in logic—which he declared he could not understand.   Dr. Arthur Charlett, appreciating the young man's antiquarian bent, persuaded him to migrate to University College, where he resided in Charlett's lodgings as a kind of amanuensis.   Later, through Charlett's aid, he was made assistant keeper of the Bodleian.[5]   There his chief task seems to have been the making of indexes to manuscript catalogues. He became very much interested in the history of

---

[1] *Ibid.*, Nos. 19, 20, 21, 22.

[2] Laws of Ethelbert, Hlothere, and Eadric, with de Laet's Latin translation.

[3] Some copies of this were printed in 1701.

[4] Prebend of Worcester.

[5] Ca. 1695.   Cf. Appendix I, No. 7.

letters, and made some collections toward a *Diplo-matica*,[1] before Hickes induced him to travel all over England in the preparation of his great catalogue, on which he seems to have been employed in the autumn of 1699.[2] This catalogue, when completed, was published as part of the *Thesaurus*, but under a separate title.[3] It contains an account of most of the then known books in any way relating to Old English, whether in manuscript or print. A history is given of each book, its age, different owners, places where kept, separate tracts in each volume, number of pages, with the opening and concluding sentences of each.

The unwieldiness and great expense of the *Thesaurus* rendered it unfit for ordinary use as a grammar.[4] In 1708 there appeared an abridgment of the grammar under the title, *Hickesii Thesauri Grammatico-Critici Conspectus Brevis*, by William Wotton. Hickes was the real editor, with some help from Wotton, and Thwaites contributed an essay on 'Saxon' coins. Some few copies of this tract were printed as gifts, under the title *Notæ in Anglo-Saxonum Nummos*. Thwaites, always a prominent helper in these 'Saxon' publications, made still another adaptation of the grammar, a much more compact and better textbook than any of its precursors. This he printed in 1711 as *Grammatica Anglo-Saxonica ex Hickesiano Thesauro excerpta*. Yet another adaptation was Miss Elstob's *Rudiments of Grammar for the Anglo-Saxon Tongue*, 1715. This is remarkable for being the first effort to

---

[1] Cf. *Ibid.*, Nos. 9, 10, 12, 15.

[2] *Ibid.*, Nos. 19, 20, 21.

[3] 'Antiquæ Literaturæ Septentrionalis Liber alter, seu Humphredi Wanleii Librorum Vett. Septentrionalium, qui in Angliæ Bibliothecis extant; nec non multorum vett. codd. Septentrionalium alibi extantium Catalogus Oxoniæ, e Theatro Sheldoniano.' 1705. Pp. 310, folio.

[4] Appendix I, Nos. 29, 30.

present the study of Old English through the medium of modern English. Unfortunately, Miss Elstob follows the old model of a Latin grammar. In 1735 Shelton translated Wotton's *Conspectus* into English.[1] The two other grammars based on Hickes are parts of dictionaries, Lye's *Grammatica Anglo-Saxonica*, appended to his edition of Junius' *Etymologicum*, 1743; and Manning's *Grammatica*, in his edition of Lye's *Dictionarium*, 1772. These are both based on the Thwaites grammar. So, quite directly, we can trace eight grammars of Old English in the eighteenth century back to the original *Institutiones* of 1689. It is hardly too much to say, then, that Hickes is responsible for both the faults and the merits of all eighteenth-century Old English scholarship. He had no predecessor in the field, for the glossary of Joscelyn and Parker eluded him, and would probably have given little aid to his plan. Bodleian MS. 33 is quoted as *Dictionariolum, sive Index Alphabeticus Vocum Saxonicarum (ni fallor) omnium, quas complectitur Grammatica clarissimi viri Dni Joannis Joscelini.*[2] For this grammar Hickes made a vain search.[3] The fragment catalogued as MS. 33—a single leaf—bears the following notation: 'Segumento interiori scriptum est "opus magistri Joselin: 1609 Mai 10" et exteriori "exeunti Anno Dom. M. DC. LXXXVIII." Hoc MS mihi dedit Johannes Batteley Archideaconus Cantuarensis. Geo Hickes.'[4]

[1] 2d edition, 1737.

[2] Wanley, p. 101.

[3] Hickes, Preface to *Institutiones*.

[4] This fragment must not be confused with the Cotton Titus A. XV and A. XVI, a Saxon-Latin glossary in two volumes; A to L, M to Z, collected out of glossaries, laws, and versions of the Gospels, Rule of St. Benedict, Gregory's *Pastoral*, Ælfric's homilies, etc., by Joscelyn and Parker.

Hickes indulged in many controversial works, and in one of these, *Several letters which passed between Dr. George Hickes and a Popish Priest*, 1705, is contained as an appendix an Old English version of Morning and Evening Prayer, translated into English by William Elstob.[1] Elstob printed one other example of Old English, the *Sermo Lupi*.[2] He and his sister Elizabeth are unique figures among Old English students. William (1673-1715) and Elizabeth (1683-1756) Elstob were related through their mother to Hickes. In childhood they were left to the care of an uncle, Charles Elstob, prebend of Canterbury. Elstob was sent away to school, but his sister, who had a remarkably quick mind, had an unhappy time until allowed to join her brother at Oxford. It was only after long pleading that she was allowed to study any languages. Arriving, as she did, at Oxford when the 'Saxonists' of Queen's were in the ascendency, she there joined her brother as a student of Old English, the enthusiasts planning to use her to teach women the language. William Elstob was consumptive, and his sister continued as his constant companion until his early death in London. Both of them acquired great skill in transcribing manuscripts, and in the art of illuminating.[3] They further had in their employ at one time a lad of ten or twelve, who had phenomenal skill as a copyist of Old English manuscripts, they being particularly interested in the homilies of Ælfric, Alfred's *Orosius*, and the *Anglo-Saxon Laws*.[4]   To consider

[1] 54 pages, Old English-English in parallel columns. Cf. Appendix III, Plate E.

[2] The Wulfstan homily, contributed to the *Thesaurus*, and also published by itself as *Sermo Lupi Episcopi*, Oxford, 1701.

[3] Among the Ballard manuscripts is a long essay by Elizabeth Elstob on this subject.

[4] The lad copied the whole of the *Textus Roffensis* in three months. This copy is now in the Antiquarian Society's collection.

their work separately for a moment, we find that William Elstob undertook the following definite contributions to Old English scholarship. First, a copy of the Junian transcript of Alfred's *Orosius*, which he translated and annotated for publication. A specimen of this was printed in 1699,[1] but was never published, probably from lack of funds. Secondly, the text and Latin translation of Wulfstan, printed twice.[2] Thirdly, a Latin version of Gregory's *Pastoral* (Ælfric's ninth homily), which was printed in his sister's edition of Gregory in 1709. Fourthly, the *Devotions of the Saxon Church*, with translation in English, printed in 1705.[3] Fifthly, a large design for an edition of the *Anglo-Saxon Laws*. The care with which the details of the edition were thought out is indicated in a draft of the proposals for printing.[4] This was to contain a corrected version of the laws published by Lambarde and Wheloc, with the addition of any others available, especially from the *Textus Roffensis;* a new Latin translation of Somner's laws; variant readings and annotations from Spelman, Selden, Junius, D'Ewes, de Laet, Hickes, etc., with the author's own notes; a preface recounting the origin and progress of English law down to Magna Charta; an historical account of each king represented as a lawmaker. Elstob's death prevented the completion of his scheme, which devolved on Wilkins.

After her brother's death, Miss Elstob disappeared from the scholarly world for at least twenty years,

---

[1] 'Hormesta Pauli Orosii quam olim patrio sermone donavit Ælfredus magnus, Anglo-Saxonum rex doctissimus. Ad exemplar Junianum edidit Wilhelmus Elstob, A. M. et Coll. Univ. Socius. Oxoniæ, e Theatro Sheldoniano.' 1699. Cf. Wanley, p. 85, and *Thesaurus*, Epistle to Shower, p. 98.

[2] Cf. note 5, p. 93.   [3] Cf. p. 93.

[4] Cf. the Ballard manuscript of *Orosius*, in the Antiquarian Society's collection.

when she was finally discovered, by some of those who remembered her remarkable scholarship, in the town of Evesham, eking out a miserable existence as mistress of a children's school, each pupil of which paid her eight groats a week. Through the interest of some of her old friends, she was made governess in the family of the Duchess of Portland, where she died at the age of seventy-three years. Not even the learned Hickes is more widely commented on by eighteenth-century literary men, and yet she dropped out of Old English scholarship forty years before her death. Perhaps the circumstances of her quaint correspondence with George Ballard, the 'mantua-maker', and worthy successor of Anthony à Wood and Thomas Hearne in the world of antiquaries, has served to heighten her importance; yet she has to her credit three rather remarkable achievements as a 'Saxonist'—the first Old English-English grammar, the first complete homily of Ælfric published with translation and notes, and the first attempt at a complete edition of Ælfric's *Homilies*. Of the grammar[1] little need be said except that it was compiled with the intention of instructing a young lady in its 'rudiments'; that the preface contains an eloquent defense of the English tongue;[2] and that a special set of Anglo-Saxon types was cast for its printing.[3] The homily on Gregory's birthday[4] was the

[1] 'The Rudiments of Grammar for the English-Saxon Tongue, First given in English: with an Apology for the Study of Northern Antiquities. Being very useful towards the understanding our ancient English Poets, and other Writers. By Elizabeth Elstob. . . . London. Printed by W. Bowyer.' 1715. 4to.

[2] Cf. Append:x II.

[3] Cf. Appendix III, p. 168.

[4] 'An English-Saxon Homily on the Birth-Day of St. Gregory: anciently used in the English Saxon Church: giving an account of the Conversion of the English from Paganism to Christianity. Translated into modern English, with notes &c., by Eliz. Elstob. London. Printed by W. Bowyer.' 1709.

joint labor of brother and sister, undertaken because
of the enthusiasm aroused by poring over William
Elstob's transcript of *Orosius*, which led her on to a
fuller study of the Old English language.[1] The proposed edition of all of Ælfric's homilies met with some
encouragement, especially from Hickes.[2] Thirty-six
pages were printed at Oxford in handsome style about
1715, but the work stopped abruptly, probably because
of her brother's death, and for lack of funds to complete the impression.[3]

The death of Hickes and Elstob within the same
year, and the consequent withdrawal of Miss Elstob
from the scholarly world, practically ended the Oxford
'Saxonists'. Thwaites had died in 1711, and the man
who gradually became leader among Oxford Old English students was of a very different calibre. Thomas
Hearne (1678-1735) was primarily an antiquary, and
not a 'Saxonist'. In the almost incredible output of
historical materials which he edited there is some
Old English, but the *Textus Roffensis* is his most notable
production in that field. This is a twelfth-century
manuscript, compiled under Bishop Ernulf, containing
miscellaneous documents and charters relating to
Rochester, and the laws of the Kentish kings. It was
probably the most widely known and frequently used
Old English manuscript in the sixteenth and seventeenth centuries. Lambarde used it in his *Archaionomia*, Spelman in the *Concilia*, Hickes in the *Thesaurus*, Harris in the *History of Kent*, and Wilkins in
the *Leges Anglo-Saxonicæ*. Twice, at least, the manuscript had been taken from the library at Rochester—
once maliciously by Dr. Leonard, who kept it two

[1] Cf. Preface to *An English-Saxon Homily*, p. 6, and Appendix II, p. 146.
[2] Cf. Appendix I, Nos. 25, 26, 27, 28.
[3] A copy is preserved in the Bodleian. The entire manuscript is in the British museum, MSS. Lansd, 370-4.

years, and only returned it after the Dean and Chapter
had sued him for its possession. Then it returned,
slightly damaged by having fallen into the water on
the way. The other occasion of its removal was for
the use of Harris while compiling his *History of Kent*,
1719. Hearne, according to his own statement, printed
the *Textus Roffensis*[1] from a transcript belonging to
Sir Edward Dering, made when the original was in
Leonard's possession. The Dean and Chapter of
Rochester, learning that their famous manuscript was
about to appear in print, threatened to stop its licens-
ing at Stationers' Hall, because it would infringe their
rights in the copy.[2] Hearne's manuscript was not a
complete text, and he added whatever he chose from
the original, excluding some of what had already appeared in print. His methods testify that the sense of
exact scholarship in reproducing originals without
abridgment or addition was not yet developed in
England.

It was characteristic of Hearne to use his various
editions as a kind of scrapbook, in which to print any
interesting bit that he chanced upon in his capacity of
under-librarian in the Bodleian. To such methods of
procedure we owe the catalogue of Joscelyn's Old
English books,[3] which Hearne inserts in his edition of
Robert of Avesbury, 1720, and to him we owe the fragment of the *Battle of Maldon* printed in John of Glas-
tonbury's *Chronicle*, 1726; the original of this fragment
perished in the Cotton fire five years later. One other

[1] 'Textus Roffensis, Accedunt, Professionum antiquorum Angliæ episco-
porum formulæ, de canonica Obedientia Archiepiscopis Cantuariensibus
præstanda, et Leonardi Hutteni Dissertatio, anglice conscripta, de Antiqui-
tatibus Oxoniensibus. E codicibus MSS. descripsit editque Tho. Hearnius.
Oxonii, e Theatro Sheldoniano.' 1720. 8°.

[2] Appendix I, No. 33.

[3] *Libri Saxonici, qui ad manus Joannis Joscelini venerunt.*

7

important document relating to Old English was published by Hearne, the *Hemingi Chartularium Ecclesiæ Wigoriensis*, 1723. Hearne began to print materials on English history in 1703, continuing throughout his life to produce works of remarkable interest and great value. One of his earlier attempts was a new edition of Spelman's *Life of Alfred*, published in English in 1709 from the original manuscript, and without the additions of Obadiah Walker. He also edited Leland's *Collectanea*, and various Middle English chronicles. His policy is rather interestingly disclosed in the preface to his edition of Robert of Gloucester: 'Fragments do not satisfy those extremely inquisitive after Books in Old English. . . . Robert of Gloucester's Chronicle is very valuable to those wishing to be acquainted with the Saxon tongue, a language which even the vulgar are very fond of talking of, though they are perfectly ignorant of it, in so much that I have known some of the Country Common People shew an unusual Pleasure when they have seen so much as the Old Saxon Letters. And 't is with great Attention that they will listen to the Derivation of Places from the Saxon Tongue.' It was his habit to ramble on in these prefaces in a way that gives much interesting antiquarian comment on subjects but slightly related to the materials in hand. This tendency toward antiquarian minutiæ was fostered by the emphasis Hickes placed upon all northern dialects in his *Thesaurus*, and by the historical notices given to manuscripts in Wanley's catalogue. One of the first evidences of this change was the revival of the Antiquarian Society.[1] Under the guidance of Wanley, Old English was henceforth to have the avowed backing of learned societies, as well as of the Universities, and

[1] Cf. Appendix IV.

increasing attention was to be paid to details relating
to the age and authenticity of manuscripts. Often-
times this attention expended itself in needless discussion, which finally brought antiquarians into dis-
favor.

David Wilkins (1685-1745) published an edition of
the *Leges Anglo-Saxonicæ*,[1] 1721, which illustrates this
increasing attention paid to the external circumstances
of manuscripts. Wilkins, who was of a German family,
had studied abroad, as well as at Oxford and Cambridge,
and was for a time librarian at Lambeth. In his edition of the laws he gives an account of the manuscripts
used, and inserts an essay, written by Nicolson,[2] that
gives a survey of all that had been done with Anglo-
Saxon laws, or was at the time known about them. To
this introduction is appended the original prefaces of
the earlier editors, Lambarde and Wheloc. As a matter
of antiquarian detail, Wilkins prints the Old English
passages occurring in his preface in a character that
seeks to reproduce the manuscript hand. The text is
in the ordinary Anglo-Saxon type used by Bowyer.
In preparing this edition, Wilkins used the *Textus Roffensis*, the Bodleian, Cotton, and Canterbury collections
of laws, in conjunction with the transcripts made by
William Elstob. This latter manuscript was in the

[1] 'Leges Anglo-Saxonicæ Ecclesiasticæ & Civiles. Accedunt Leges
Edvardi Latinæ, Guilielmi Conquestoris Gallo-Normannicæ, et Henrici 1
Latinæ, subjungitur Domini Henr. Spelmanni Codex Legum Veterum Stat-
utorum Regni Angliæ, quæ ab ingressu Guilielmi 1 usque ad annum nonum
Henr. III. edita sunt. Toti Operi præmittitur Dissertatio Epistolaris ad-
modum Reverendi Domini Guilielmi Nicolsoni Episcopi Derrensis de Jure
Feudali Veterum Saxonum. Cum Codd. MSS. contulit, Notas, Versionem
& Glossarium adjecit David Wilkins, S. T. P. Canonicus Cantuariensis,
Reverendissimo in Christo Patri ac Domino Guilielmo Divina Providentia
Archiepiscopo Cantuariensi, &c, &c. a Sacris Domesticis & Biblioth.' Lon-
don, 1721, fol.

[2] Seventeen pages in length.

possession of Elizabeth Elstob, who seems to have been very loth to part with it, and it did not come into Wilkins' possession soon enough to aid him materially.[1] The Anglo-Saxon laws themselves cover 195 folio pages, double columns of Old English with Latin translation; these are followed by nearly twice as many laws in Latin. The whole work is supplied with a glossary and a good index. Wilkins professes to have lost a hundred pounds by this edition—the expense of gathering his materials. Yet it had an imposing list of subscribers, and was greatly aided by Bishop Nicolson.[2] In the first column of his *Concilia Magnæ Britanniæ*, 1737, Wilkins makes further use of charters, decrees, and extracts from the *Anglo-Saxon Chronicle*. In addition to his own elaborate works, he found time to edit Selden's complete works, 1725-6.[3]

Thwaites died a decade before George Smith (1693-1756) completed his father's edition of Bede, yet the influence of his scholarship is visible in that work. John Smith (1659-1715) was a Cambridge man, and although he held various ecclesiastical preferments, he spent much of his time at the University, working on an elaborate edition of the *Historia Ecclesiastica*, which had been first printed by Wheloc. This he did not live to complete. In the meantime, his son George became a student of Old English under Thwaites at Queen's College, Oxford, where his uncle, Joseph Smith, was Provost. The younger man applied his knowledge of the language to the careful editing of his father's pa-

---

[1] Cf. Nicolson's *Correspondence*.

[2] Cf. letters of Wilkins to Nicolson in Nicolson's *Correspondence*. It would appear that Nicolson had given a pension to help him in the undertaking.

[3] *Johannis Seldeni Jurisconsulti Opera Omnia, tam edita quam inedita*. London, 1725-6, 3 vols., fol.

pers, and the book appeared in 1722.[1] To the text as printed by Wheloc, Smith adds a Latin preface, giving the sources of his material, and some account of the previous uses made of Bede: and he adds a Latin life of Bede. This book was printed at Cambridge—the first Old English work of any importance printed at that University for seventy-five years. For its printing, Cambridge procured a new font of Anglo-Saxon types.[2]

The same year, at Oxford, Francis Wise (1695-1767) brought out a new edition of Asser's *Ælfredi Vita*.[3] This has proved an interesting book to modern students, because it furnishes the only means of comparing the Parker edition of 1574 with the original manuscript. Wise printed from this manuscript, which was destroyed in the Cotton fire; and, by comparing the two editions, it has been possible partly to disentangle the original manuscript-sources from Parker's interpolations.[4] He has also preserved a specimen of the original manuscript-hand—but, unlike Parker, he prints this Latin life in Roman characters. To this he appends Alfred's Old English preface to Gregory's *Pastoral Care*. Wise was a man of far more scholarly attainment than the men who immediately succeeded him as editors. He was intimately acquainted with the libraries of Oxford, where, after taking his degree at Trinity, he became first an under-librarian at the

---

[1] 'Historiæ Ecclesiasticæ Gentis Anglorum Libri quinque, auctore Sancto & Venerabili Bæda Presbytero Anglo-Saxone. Una cum reliquis ejus Operibus Historicis in unum Volumen collectis, Cura et studio Johannis Smith, S. T. P. et Ecclesiæ Dunelmensis non ita pridem canonici, Cantabrigiæ Typis Academicis.' 1722, fol.

[2] Cf. Appendix III.

[3] 'Annales rerum gestarum Ælfredi Magni, auctore Asserio Menevensi recensuit Franciscus Wise, A. M. Coll. Trin. Soc. Oxonii.' 1722, 8°.

[4] Cf. Stevenson, *Asser's Life of King Alfred*, Oxford, 1904.

Bodleian, and then for many years the head of the Radcliffe library. He was on terms of intimate friendship with Charlett, who, he says, urged him to undertake the edition of Asser.

Dr. Arthur Charlett, who died in 1722 at the age of about 67, was Master of University College for thirty years, during which period he witnessed the whole career of the 'Oxford Saxonists'. He was born, probably, the year that Junius published Cædmon, and came to Oxford about the time that Marshall returned as head of Lincoln College. From then until his death he was closely associated with all the 'Saxonists', and had voluminous correspondence with them.[1] He never undertook to edit any Old English, but gave great encouragement to all activities in that branch of scholarship. His name appears among various lists of subscribers to Old English publications, for he was noted for his generosity, in spite of a very slender purse. With him we may include, as a patron of the 'Saxonists', Thomas Tanner (1674-1735), a Queen's College man, contemporary with Thwaites. He was Prebend of Ely, Archdeacon of Norwich, Canon of Christ Church, Oxford, and Bishop of St. Asaph. In these various preferments he gathered a remarkable library—especially at Norwich—and at his death left the whole of it to Oxford. It is recorded that his collections arrived in seven cart-loads about three months after his death.[2] His great work *Bibliotheca Britannico-Hibernica*, was published by Bishop Wilkins in 1748. Among 'Oxford Saxonists', Tanner and Wanley will ever stand out as the founders of encyclopædic works on early English books.

The roll of the 'Saxonists' of Queen's would not be

---

[1] Cf. Appendix III, Nos. 14, 15, 20, 21, 22, 27, 28, 29, 30, 31, 32.

[2] Cf. Madan, *Catalogue of Western Manuscripts*, Vol. 3.

complete without some mention of John Hudson (d. 1719). He started his career as a serving-child at Queen's when only fourteen. Later he became fellow of University College, 1684, and a noted tutor in Greek. As librarian at the Bodleian, 1701, he did not get on well with Wanley, nor, later, with Hearne, with whom he quarreled over political matters. Hudson was a zealous guardian of the Bodleian treasures, and never allowed his 'Saxonist' friends any liberties there. He spent much of his time in compiling a catalogue of the library's printed books, but did not live to complete it.

Before considering the last group of Old English scholars in the eighteenth century, we may briefly sum up what this earlier group had accomplished, from Marshall's return to Oxford in 1668 to the death of Gibson in 1748. The greatest results belong to the end of the seventeenth century, when, as we have seen, the activities centred in making grammars;[1] printing hitherto unedited texts;[2] revising the work of earlier editors;[3] and completing and editing the unfinished works of previous scholars.[4] Aside from these, there was a continuation of the historical collections, such as we find in Dugdale.[5] After the publication of the *Thesaurus*, we see the interest growing in catalogues, encyclopædic accounts of materials, attention to small details, and the desire to give as much and varied information as possible on any subject allied to the material printed. In this we see the first indication of the methods of modern scholarship, but imbedded in a naïve interest which attaches to the collector rather than to the true editor.

[1] Marshall, Nicolson, Hickes.
[2] Thwaites, Rawlinson, Elstob.
[3] Benson, Gibson.
[4] Wharton, Brome, Gibson.
[5] Wharton, Gale.

A glance at some of the projected works of this period shows how active were preparations for great books, most of which failed for lack of pecuniary support:

1692. Wanley: *Abridgement of Somner's Dictionary.*[1]
1697. J. Smith: *Anglo-Saxon Charters.*[2]
1698. Thwaites: *Orosius.*[3]
1699. Elstob: *Orosius.*[4]
1705. Wanley: *Old English Bible.*[5]
1705. Elstob: *Anglo-Saxon Laws.*[6]
1705. Hickes: *Cædmon.*[7]
1709. E. Elstob: *Psalter.*[8]
1715. E. Elstob: *Ælfric's Homilies.*[9]

By the middle of the century Old English scholarship waned. There were then only three men whose publications increased the bulk of Old English printed books—Lye, Manning, and Barrington.

Edward Lye (1694-1767) was an Oxford man, who grew very enthusiastic over the study of Gothic and Old English. In 1743 he edited and published the elaborate *Etymologicum*[10] of Francis Junius, which had lain in the Bodleian nearly three-quarters of a century. To this he made several additions before publishing— such as an outline of Old English and Gothic grammar, which he based on the grammar of Hickes, and a life of the author. This remained for a long time the basis

[1] MS. Harl. 3317.
[2] Cotton Manuscripts.
[3] Cf. *Gentleman's Magazine*, Sept., 1834.
[4] MS. Lansd. 373.
[5] MS. Harl. 3777, Art. 162.
[6] MS. Harl. 3780, Art. 134.
[7] MS. Harl. 3777, Art. 162.
[8] Cf. Appendix I, No. 25.
[9] MS. Lansd. 370-4.

[10] 'Francisci Junii Francisci Filii, Etymologicum Anglicanum, ex autographo descripsit & accessionibus permultis auctum edidit Edwardus Lye A. M. . . . Præmittuntur Vita auctoris et Grammatica Anglo-Saxonica. Oxonii: e Theatro Sheldoniano.' 1743, fol.

of all Old English philology. Lye began compiling an Old English dictionary of his own, for which proposals were issued the year of his death. This was to be in 'Saxon' and English, 'a work never before attempted', so the proposal states. To this was to be added a 'specimen of the theology, bequests, grants, and poetry of the Anglo-Saxons'. The edition was to be limited to two hundred copies, quarto, to sell at one guinea. Most of this was adapted from Hickes and Junius, and remained unedited until 1772, when it came out under the direction of Owen Manning (1721-1801), a Cambridge man, who also printed *King Alfred's Will*, 1788.[1] Manning was not a remarkable scholar, nor was the dictionary up to the general expectation of it, although its publication was heralded as a long-awaited treasure. Lye had worked hard in preparing his dictionary, but the death of Lord Granville, his patron, so discouraged him that he was for abandoning it; however, Archbishop Secker urged him on, and he was especially cheered by the reception his proposals met with in Germany. It is therefore interesting to consider the list of subscribers, many of whom had subscribed to Lye's work. In the list, one reads of eleven colleges in Cambridge and seven in Oxford, beside Eton, Edinburgh, and Windsor. Three copies went to a bookseller in Leyden, and one to Göttingen University. The work came out in two volumes, under Manning's supervision.[2] No further attempt at an Old English dictionary was made in the eighteenth century.

[1] Junius MS. 15, which was transcribed from Cott. MS. Tib. B. 1.

[2] 'Dictionarium Saxonico et Gothico-Latinum. Auctore Edvardo Lye, A. M. Rectore de Yardley-Hastings in Agro Northantoniensi. Accedunt fragmenta Versionis Ulphilanæ, nec non Opuscula quædam Anglo-Saxonica. Edidit nonnullis vocabulis auxit, plurimis exemplis illustravit, et Grammaticam utriusque Linguæ præmisit Owen Manning.' London, 1772, 2 vols., fol.

Daines Barrington (1727-1800), of Brasenose College, Oxford, at last succeeded in publishing the oft-
attempted *Orosius*. Barrington was a lawyer, and a
member of the Society of Antiquaries. For his edition
he used Elstob's transcript of *Orosius*, which was copied
from the Junian transcript.[1] The Elstob transcript had
been sold, after his death, to Joseph Ames, who thought
of publishing it, and from Ames it was purchased by
Samuel Pegge, in the hope that Manning would undertake the editing. Upon his refusal, Pegge turned to
Barrington. On his own confession, Barrington failed
to collate his manuscript with the original, on the excuse of the careful work done by both Junius and Elstob. He further admits having altered the spelling
and punctuation, to suit his own ideas of clearness and
propriety. The variant readings he gives, only because
their omission would be discourteous to the industry of
the antiquaries who made the transcripts. One comment in his preface is suggestive of the state of Old
English scholarship near the end of the eighteenth
century. He says: 'There are so few who concern
themselves about Anglo-Saxon literature that I have
printed the work chiefly for my own amusement, and
that of a few antiquarian friends'. He declares that
his reasons for printing the translations and notes in
English are based on his recognition of the near affinity
of the old and modern forms of the language, and excuses the long adherence to Latin editions of Old English works on the ground that for foreign scholars, in
preceding centuries, when English was little known on
the Continent, Latin was more easily understood than
English could be.

The dignity of the English language was greatly

[1] 'The Anglo-Saxon Version, from the Historian Orosius. By Alfred
the Great. Together with an English Translation from the Anglo-Saxon.'
London, 1773.

increased in 1755 by Samuel Johnson's dictionary. In his preface he makes extensive use of passages from Early English writers, chronologically arranged, beginning with Alfred's *Boethius*, and continuing down to Sir J. Wilson (1553). The popularity of anything written by Johnson, and the many editions of his dictionary, containing the essay on the history of the English language, had a definite effect upon Old English studies in two ways: first, it increased the respect for the use of modern English as a medium of translation; and, secondly, it so aroused interest in modern English studies as to lessen the interest in Old English. Warton, in his *History of English Poetry*, declared Old English to be jejune, scoffed at its literary value, and refused to consider it seriously. The Society of Antiquaries were too busy splitting hairs over inscriptions and coins and antiquarian novelties to further any serious editions of Old English texts. When, in 1753, an edition of *Cædmon* was proposed by Edward Rowe Mores, the Society refused to bear the expense of engraving plates from the original drawings of Junius. This edition of *Cædmon* was to have been the joint labor of Lye and Wise—the one to translate the text, the other to describe the manuscript and its dialects. In spite of the fact that a bookseller was found who was willing to pay the expense of printing, if relieved of the engravings, the project fell through.

It is hard to assign any causes for the rapid decline of interest in Old English in the second half of the eighteenth century. After an unusually brilliant period in any literary movement, there is an inevitable decline. It was true after Chaucer; it was equally true after the Elizabethan age. Old English scholarship had its period of greatest activity at the time when Dryden was literary dictator. The period of Dr. Johnson, of Oliver Goldsmith, and of the eighteenth-century novelists, is one that tends to social expression rather than to minute scholarship, and since there were no controversies, civil or religious, in which it could serve as testimony, Old English had no place in Georgian England, which did not as yet recognize the literary treasures existing in the early language.

There was a general sense of depression in the Universities, scholarship was at a low ebb, and the unacademic world regarded Old English with suspicion, since they could not read its strange characters, nor plod through the stilted Latin translations. If Old English was in danger of sinking into oblivion at the death of Parker in the sixteenth century, it was in far greater danger of sinking beneath contempt at the end of the eighteenth century. Two circumstances saved it: one was the appearance of Sharon Turner's *History of the Anglo-Saxons*, 1799-1805, which, by connecting the history and the literature of their ancestors, roused in the English a new sense of patriotic pride in all the records of that early period. The other, and even more fortunate circumstance, was the establishment of an Old English professorship at Oxford. Such a lectureship had been provisionally tried in the seventeenth century under Thwaites, but was operative only so long as his personal enthusiasm was there to guide the students. Again, in 1720, we find Gibson corresponding with Charlett relative to some new plan for such a foundation.[1] About this time Richard Rawlinson (16⅜⅜ to 1755), son of Sir Thomas Rawlinson, Lord Mayor of London, was receiving an honorary D. C. L. from Oxford. Rawlinson was particularly proud of this degree, and it is not unlikely that, wishing to confer some favor on his own college, St. John's, he made a tentative proposal of a lectureship in 'Saxon'. This seems the more probable because later, when he ac-

---

[1] Appendix I, No. 32.

tually provided for such a foundation, there was little incentive to consider 'Saxon' studies, because the great students of the language were dead. Rawlinson had been at Oxford in the days of Thwaites, Hickes, and Charlett, and his enthusiasm as a book-collector led him to an intimate knowledge of antiquities. In 1750 he made known his intention of establishing a professorship in Anglo-Saxon. During the next five years of his life, his personal peculiarities led him to add first one codicil, then another, until he had greatly restricted the tenure. No professor was to be appointed for forty years after his death; St. John's College was to have the first and every fifth succeeding appointment, the tenure to be five years; members of the Antiquarian Society were to be excluded as candidates. As a result of these restrictions, the choice was greatly narrowed, and did not always admit of the appointment of the best man. Charles Mayo, Fellow of St. John's, was the first Rawlinsonian professor. Apparently he knew very little about Old English. The wheel, however, was set in motion—there did exist a properly endowed and definitely planned professorship in Old English—a foundation from which has gradually risen the whole system of University study in English. The Rawlinsonian professorship has existed now for one hundred and twenty years, and the undue restrictions have long since been removed. Cambridge was soon to follow the example of Oxford, and the universities of other nations after them, in establishing Old English as a separate and distinct part of collegiate training.

At the end of the eighteenth century the students of Old English had the equipment for scientific study. Great treasures of manuscripts had been collected, and were reasonably accessible; there were catalogues of the various collections, especially the comprehensive and

painstaking work of Wanley; grammars and dictionaries had been published; a considerable body of the
more important prose was already in print; and means
of further study was supplied by the newly established
Rawlinsonian professorship. The task of nineteenth-
century students was to systematize these materials,
and evolve a scientific basis for the study of Old English.

At the opening of the nineteenth century, England
had become a treasure-house for continental scholars.
Notable among these were the Scandinavians, Rask
and Thorkelin, and, among Germans, the brothers
Grimm. Rask will long be remembered as a pioneer
among scientific grammarians, while Thorkelin was the
first foreign scholar of the century to engage extensively
in promoting the publication of Old English texts.
To the mass of materials already collected by English
scholars, as well as to the very faults of the earlier
grammarians and lexicographers, the Germanic philologists are greatly indebted in their scientific research
—a task for which they were peculiarly adapted by
national temperament, and by their superior knowledge
of all the Teutonic dialects. The English scholars still
clung to the methods of their predecessors, both in
their editorial efforts and in their instruction. It soon
became apparent that there was to be a new and an
old school of 'Saxonists'. Between these factions feeling ran so high as to render most undignified and un-
scholarly the articles in that famous controversy
known as 'the Gentleman's Magazine quarrel', which
reached its climax about 1834. This date may be taken,
approximately, as the end of the system of Old English
study built up by the generations of English theologians and antiquaries from Matthew Parker to George
Hickes. The impetus for English investigators had
always been controversial or antiquarian; to them the

stronger appeal lay in the contents of early literature, not in linguistic study. Perhaps in this fact lies the ultimate reason why the application of exact, scientific methods of linguistic study has been more vigorously pursued by foreign than by British students of Old English.

The ethnic and political history of the British Isles furnishes a unique chapter in the evolution of language. First we have an untutored race, the Anglo-Saxons, bringing with them little or no knowledge of letters, imposing their language on the prehistoric Britons, who have left us no records save in their conquerors' tongue. Scarcely had the language thus acquired taken shape when it suffered further modifications through the Danish invasion. Within three centuries thereafter, the Normans had so far discouraged the English language that it became practically the language of the illiterate, preserved among learned men only as a means of communication with the unlettered. By the time that modern English had emerged triumphant as a literary language in the writings of Chaucer, the English of the Anglo-Saxons was a dead language, and long before its resurrection by the English Reformers, all oral tradition of its structure had perished. What, then, does the effort to revive a knowledge of Old English signify in the history of literature?

The most immediate effect of the revival was on legal and historical knowledge. This naturally affected the style of what we may call non-literary prose—historical, legal, and theological writings. We may further suspect that the peculiar grace and nervous vigor of eighteenth-century prose is largely indebted to the rediscovery of the simplicity of the mother-tongue. Miss Elstob laid great emphasis on the force of monosyllables in the 'Saxon', and called attention to their use by Dryden, Pope, and Prior. It is not to be in-ferred from this that these men of letters were themselves careful students of the early language; but we can readily believe that literary men, from Ben Jonson (who included a 'Saxon' alphabet in his *English Grammar*) to Samuel Johnson (who borrowed so extensively from the *Etymologicum* of Junius in his English Dictionary), were peculiarly sensitive to the distinctive qualities of Old English. Nowhere is this permeating influence of the rediscovery of Old English to be seen more clearly than in the numerous English grammars, which, to the days of Lindley Murray, included specimen alphabets, paradigms, and remarks on the 'Saxon' tongue. We have already called attention to the fact that Old English scholarship was most productive in the time of Dryden. This gives food for reflection on the possible connection of the Old English revival with what has long been regarded as a highly Latinized prose. Dryden himself, at times, exhibits an ease of style that is not Latin. Sir Thomas Browne, in his own quaint way, writes an essay on the 'Saxon' tongue, and Selden's delightful *Table Talk* is the work of a man saturated with the spirit of Old English manuscripts. A less immediate result of the Old English revival is to be found in nineteenth-century poets and novelists. This influence can best be estimated if we pause to consider what we should lose if wholly ignorant of the *Anglo-Saxon Chronicle;* the writings of King Alfred; the wealth of romance in *Beowulf;* the ingenuity of the Early English chroniclers.

Thus we are led to conclude that to Old English scholars between 1566 and 1800 we owe, first, the preservation of many priceless manuscripts, and the knowledge of their whereabouts; next, the preservation, through transcripts, of many originals which have perished. These two things alone put us heavily in debt to the elder scholars. The results of their scholarly labors, too, were not in vain, for no exact science can spring full-grown from its conception. In Old English, as in other fields, much has been learned from the very mistakes of the pioneers. Doubtless there was some truth in Barrington's assertion about Latin-Old English translations; the interest of Continental scholars would have been harder to gain, with an unfamiliar tongue to explain an unknown language. Above all, we must remember that Old English scholarship had its beginnings parallel with the greatest age in English poetry— that it, too, was Elizabethan. Undoubtedly it swelled that wave of patriotic fervor which breaks so marvelously in the works of Spenser and Shakespeare. We may further suppose that the study of Old English manuscripts for two centuries and a half by the most cultivated theologians, lawyers, and antiquaries has incalculably modified the prose diction of our language, and contributed subtle nourishment to that vigor and simplicity which our mother-tongue has in its best and purest expression.

APPENDIX I

The following extracts from letters are arranged chronologically. They are included because they throw considerable light on the difficulties and progress of Old English scholarship for the century of its greatest activity in England (1624-1720). Nos. 8, 11, 16, 17, 18, 21, 22, 23, 24, 28, 31, from the Rawlinson and Ballard collections, are printed directly from the manuscripts.

(1)

Dr. James Ussher to Sir Robert Cotton[1]

(Proposes to collect the history of the 'Saxon' Church.)

When it shall please God to restore me to my health, I will endeavour to recompence what is past, not only in continueing the History of the Brittish, Scottish, and Irish beyond the yeare 600 (where I purposed to stint my selfe) untill the year 1000: but also (if it shall so seem good to his Ma^(tie)) to collect the history of the Saxon Church, untill the comeing of the Normannes. To you only am I, and must be more beholding for furnishing me with materialls, for which I professe I am unable to render you condigne thankes, and therefore must leave that requitall to his Ma^(ty) who setteth me on work.[2]
Dec. 20, 1624.

(2)

Sir William Boswell to Sir Simonds D'Ewes[3]

(Concerning Old English Vocabularies.)

I have often thought how much the knowledge of this present Low-Dutch language would advantage your intelligence of our old Saxon (if your study enclineth still that way:) but you are best able to think what will be most

[1] Cott. MS. Jul. C. 111, fol. 156, and Ellis, *Letters of Eminent Literary Men*, London, 1843, No. 41.

[2] Ussher, under the commission of King James, published *Britannicarum Ecclesiarum Antiquitates*, in 1639.

[3] Harl. MS. 374, fol. 92, and Ellis, No. 53.

propre for you. I should long ere this have sent you a
Transcript of the Saxon Vocabularie, you had once of mee;
but that it is collected only out of the four Evangelists,
and one or two other small things, printed in that tongue;
and farr short of a Dictionarie with (our honorable frend)
Sr Thomas Cotton, made by Jocelinis (Secretarie sometime
to Mathewe Parker Archbishop of Canterbury, and com-
piler of Antiquitates Ecclesiæ Britannicæ) and one of
another Dictionarie, which I think Mr Lisle of the Isle of
Ely (whom I think you know to be extraordinarily skilfull
in that language), would have printed, long since, of his
owne gathering.[1]

Dec. 18, 1636.

(3)

Abraham Wheloc to D'Ewes[2]

*(Recommending ' Saxon' studies as elucidating early
church doctrines.)*

Most learned and trulie noble Sir, how much I am
bound to serve you, your most quickninge and effectual letters shew. I would faine come over to doe my personal humble service to your worship; but in truth my twofold imploy-
ment, of the Arabick one, and the other of the Brittish
and Saxon Ecclesiastical and Political Antiquities (to which
latter by Sir H. Spelman I am now designed,) besides
other studies, cause me against my will to stay here by it;
in these studies of Antiquities I acknowledge your rare
and incomparable progresse, though I am keeper of the
University bookes, yet not of such treasures as you have
gathered. I could wish that our learned gentrie (if peace
continue) would imploy some scholars to be under them
(and myselfe though most unworthy of that honor would
willinglie be one) to compile a body of our Divinity, I say
of our doctrine out of the Saxon and Brittish writers: and
to præsent the papists with these, as a rule to leade them
by, if they would be constant to the best Antiquities.
Most sure it is, that Antiquitie tells us we owe more to
the Easterne Church than to Rome. . . . What Augustin
did concerninge the slaughter of Bangor Monkes, with the
blessed Mr Fox I say, I cannot tel. Of six ould Manuscripts three in Latin, and three in Saxon, I have the use,

---

[1] Boswell was then secretary to the English Ambassador at the Hague,
where he wrote this letter.

[2] Harl. MS. 374, fol. 129, and Ellis, No. 57.

and all the three Lattin agree that then Augustin was deade. The Saxon all of K: Alureds indeede, leaves out the passage. From that we must not argue; for that is usual in every line almost, as also to adde now and then.

Sir, I will cause any thinge to be transcribed out of Trinity College, their Ælfric: they are many: and not all of the same publick mindes: though it may befor a fortnight I may cause it to be sent you: and I shall try what may be doone, if doone without noise.

Sʳ Thomas Cotton (to whom as yet I am scarce knowne, and yet because trusted in Cambridge, he alsoe trusteth me,) he is of a very sweete demeanure; and takes it an honor to himselfe and familie, to serve our noble and learned gentrie, with his rare Antiquities, and that in his owne name. If your Worship will not appeare your selfe in borrowing any thinge of him (which may paradventure greive him) yet I may use your name, and soe doe that way what I can; though impossible sure to borrow that choicest monument; fitting it is you should have a coppie of the best of them; and Sir Thomas wondered that not more did come thither, and transcribe them. I am sure this he sayd to me, or to this effect. I shall ever studie to serve your Worship to the utmost of my power, and soe at this present I humbly commit you to the gracious protection of the Almightie.

Jan. 26, 1639.

(4)

SIR HENRY SPELMAN TO WHELOC[1]

(*Concerning the 'Saxon' lecture at Cambridge.*)

I have acquainted my Lord's Grace of Armagh[2] and my Lord Bishop of Elye,[3] with the intended Lecture, and have entreated them severally to consider of the manner of setling of it, to confer with Mr Vice-chanceler[4] and the Heades whom they thinke good about it; which it hath pleased them very willingly to undertake. I made a draughte of my Intente touching the manner of conveyinge from me and my sonne, to be considered of by Counsell for the Universitie, and to be proceeded in as they shall advise, and I shewed it to my L.L. of Armagh and Ely. But my Lord of Ely is not like to be in Cambridge while

---

[1] Harl. Ms. 7041, fol. 90, and Ellis, No. 59. [3] Matthew Wren.

[2] James Ussher. [4] John Cosin.

my Lord of Armagh is there, and therefore he reserved
the perusing of it till you brought it to him afterward.
They both have promised me to grace you with their
favour and assistance. But the approbation and choice of
Mr Vicechanceler and the Heads must be principally hadd
therewith. I send you a Coppy of the Draught to shew
to Mr Vicechanceler, with tender of my service. But I
pray divulge it not to common discourse. I also shewed
my Lord of Armagh your intended Speech, and left it with
his Lordship to peruse, but have no censure from him.
I feare it will neither like him nor your Auditory in respect
of some obscurity, intricacie, and the length. Nor do I
delight to be talked on *ex rostris*. More hereafter. Thus
mutch in haste. Farewell.

June 26, 1640.

(5)

WILLIAM DUGDALE TO D'EWES[1]

(*Commending Somner.*)

I hope now that you have the advantage of that honest
man Mr Sumner his helpe, you will speede the impression
of your Saxon Lexicon and the Laws. Those noe doubt
will goe of much better, though the times be bad, than
Beda, which you know was printed in the heat of the
Warr. I pray you thinke well thereof, and neglect not
this opportunity of Mr Sumners helpe, who as he hath
otherwise assisted you much, soe may he correct the presse,
which will be an especiall matter.[2]

Jan. 2, 1649.

(6)

SIR JOHN COTTON TO DR. THOMAS SMITH[3]

(*Concerning the Cotton Library.*)

I received your letter, and return you very many
thanks for your kind proposals concerning my library.
Truly, Sir, we are fallen into so dangerous times, that it
may be more for my private concerns, and the public, too,

[1] Harl. MS. 374, fol. 294, and Ellis, No. 68.

[2] D'Ewes never published any Old English, but was designed by Spelman to prepare a dictionary. His collections towards this end were given to Somner.

[3] Bliss, *Letters Written by Eminent Persons in the Seventeenth and Eighteenth Centuries,* London, 1813, No. 8.

that the library should not be too much known. There are many things in it, which are very cross to the Romish interest, and you know what kind of persons the Jesuits are. My little villa at Stratton is now very pleasant; if you please (whilst your college is now in trouble) to make this place your retreat, you shall be most heartily welcome, and then we shall have time to discourse of this and other affairs. Pray forget not to present my service to Sir W. Hayward.

June 30, 1687.

(7)

SMITH TO HUMPHRY WANLEY[1]

(Commending Wanley's 'Saxon' studies.)

I am very glad of the new post you are preferred to, as you write, the publick Library.[2] If in turning over the Greek Catenas upon the books of Scripture, you light upon any fragments of S. Irenæus, . . . or any other writer of the sixth or seventh century, . . . you will oblige me by the communication of such notices. But let this be done without prejudice to your study of the Saxon language and antiquities, which seem to be your peculiar province, and which I would have you cultivate with your utmost industry.

Feb. 22, 169⅞.

(8)

EDMUND GIBSON TO EDWARD THWAITES[3]

(Concerning the Pentateuch.)

By a letter from Dr Mills, I percieve you begin to resume the thoughts of publishing the Pentateuch, in Saxon. Had we a Collection of all ye Texts of Scripture y^t are occasionally quoted in ye Homilies, it might be conveniently joyn'd to your design: And if you should run over ye Homilies for y^t purpose, I hope you'l have an eye to all ye passages against Popery. I doubt not, by what I have had an opportunity of seeing, but a collection of that kind would be pretty large; and it would be an undeniable evidence to all posterity, that the belief of our

---

[1] Harl. MS. 3782, Art. 45, and Ellis, No. 102.

[2] Smith was Cottonian Librarian, Wanley just appointed to the Bodleian.

[3] Rawl. MS. D. 377.

Papists at this day, is a very different thing from that of
our Saxon-Ancestors. If I am able to do you any service
in these parts, you may freely command.

May 20, 1697.

(9)

SMITH TO WANLEY[1]

(Concerning the loan of MSS. from the Cottonian.)

As to what concernes the other part of your letter, I
must take leave to write freely to you, that I am extremely
amazed at your request of having the book of the Charters
of the Saxon Kings[2] . . . sent down to Oxon, upon a
more than single accompt. Truly if the mountaine cannot
come to Mahomet, Mahomet must condescend and be
content to go to the mountaine. I believe, that that curious
and invaluable booke was never lent out of the house since
the Collection was first made, no not to Mr Selden, nor to
Sir William Dugdale, tho' they had the free use of the
Library as much as if it had been their owne: and for my
own part I was forced to use it there, and to go downe to
Westminster, tho' indisposed, and in all weathers, when I
made that hasty and imperfect extract of it, without so
much as presuming to bee favoured with the use of it at
my lodging, which would have been at that time a great
ease and advantage to mee. I beeleive also, that by all
the interest which you have in the man in whose lodgings
you are, you would not be able, tho' I should desire it, to
procure that a book or two bee lent me out of the Museum
Ashmoleanum, much less out of the Bodleyan Library;
which, besides other conveniences, would save me the
expense and trouble of a journey to Oxon; nor indeed could
I obtain leave of myselfe to make such a request of the
Vice-Chancellor if the thing were feasible. Besides you
could not possibly forget, when you wrote your letter, by
referring to my preface, in which I mention several other
Charters of the Saxon Kings in the boxes of the Library
(which I am fully satisfyed, that no man now alive knew
of but myself, I made the discovery) that tho' I did not
make an absolute promise of publishing those Charters,
and the formes of the old letters found in them, and in
other antient books; yet as I had at that time, so now at
this present I have the same designe and resolution to

---

[1] Harl. MS. 3782, Art. 49, and Ellis, No. 105.

[2] Cott. MS. Aug. 1.

publish them with several other pieces of antiquity, when
a fit opportunity shall present itself. But this I say upon
a supposition, that if by the misfortune of the times I be
driven out of London, or be hindered by the infirmityes of
my age, and the other circumstances of my life, from per-
forming those serious intentions, I shall then readily and
willingly devolve that work upon you. In the mean while
you would do well to examine and transcribe whatever is
of this nature in the publick Library where you are fixed,
and where you have such happy opportunityes of study,
which I believe would take up more time than you may
at first imagine, without seeking for materialls abroad;
and after this, when I see that to finish your great undertaking you have procured charters and other records and
monuments of antiquity out of the Library of St. James's,
of Lambeth, and of Corpus Christi College in Cambridge
(and why not, to make your book absolutely perfect, out
of the Tower of London or Exchequer at Westminster?) it
will be a great motive to prevail with Sir J. Cotton to com-
ply with your request, and a much greater with mee, to
give up wholly into your hands the credit of such a vast
undertaking.[1] Consider well your own strength, and what
burden you are able to beare, that you may not sinke under
it. . . . If you take amiss my free way of writing in this
particular matter, perchance you will wrong yourself: but
if you thinke that it proceeds from any distrust I have of
you, or unwillingness to oblige you in what I may or can,
you will extremely wrong mee. For I assure you that I
have a great value, respect, and kindness for you.
June 8, 1697.

(10)

WANLEY TO SMITH[2]

(A scheme for a history of letters.)

I am very sorry I should mention the borrowing of that
book of the Saxon Charters to you, seeing it cannot be
lent out, and humbly crave your pardon for my rashness;
and tho' there are many other books in that noble library
which would be useful to me in my present design, (which
is more relating to the nature of Letters, than to the Diplo-
mata or Charters themselves,) yet I shall not for the future,

[1] Wanley planned a treatise on the various characters of manuscripts;
this was not completed. Smith did not publish his charters.

[2] Bliss, No. 34.

make use [of] any of my friends to get them hither, but content myself till I can go to London. To unfold my meaning a little further, my intent is to trace the Greek and Latin letters from the oldest monuments of antiquity now extant, as the marbles and medals, to the MSS. and so down to the present age. When any other language derives its character from these as the Coptic or Russian from the Greek; the Francic, Irish, Saxon, &c. from the Latin, I shall consider them in their several times, but the Saxon I would especially bring down from the oldest Charters to the present English hands.[1] The Charters I believe may be older than the books, and may determine the age of all the Saxon MSS. with the assistance of some other remarks, but one cannot rely upon them, till we know for certain which be genuine and which not; and to find this a man had need of the help of altogether, this made me so bold as to desire the book. I am not in haste with my design, which I know will cost many years time, and the trouble of a personal view of every book in capital letters in Europe, &c. yet after all, if nobody shall in that time have prevented me, I may have a second vol. *de re Anglorum diplomatica*, which I pray God grant you health and opportunity to give the world, since undoubtedly you are the most capable of any man now living to do.
June 20, 1697.

(11)

WILLIAM NICOLSON TO THWAITES[2]

(*Concerning the Bible in Old English.*)

I was some time agoe acquainted (by yr good friend and mine, Mr Gibson) that you were designing an Edition of the Saxon pentateuch; and, by the last post, I had a Specimen of ye Book from Mr Elstob. You will easily imagine how much I am pleas'd to see yt sort of Learning flourish; and how ready I shall alwaies be to give it the outmost furtherance that a man in my circumstances can doe. I gave Mr Gibson, some years agoe, a small fragment of such a version of Exodus; wch I presume he has communicated to you. I have not hitherto been able to retrieve ye remaining parts of yt and ye other four Books; tho' I do not yet despair of it. But—the various Readings would not be many (if we may judge by this Scrap) that the whole would afford us; and therfore the want of such

---

[1] The partial results of this scheme were embodied in Hickes' *Thesaurus*.

[2] MS. Rawl. D. 377, fol. 41a.

an entire Copy is the less considerable. I need not tell you that, in the Preface to K. Ælfred's Laws, we have not onely the Decalogue already publish'd fro yᵉ 20ᵗʰ of Exodus; but most of the three following Chapters, and some other portions of the Jewish Law, wherein perhaps the printed Copy may differ from your Manuscript. You will give me leave to subscribe for a dozen Copies of yʳ Book. The money shall be sent as you shall direct.

I lately sent Mr. Elstob a Runic Inscription wᶜʰ I desired he might communicate to you, and whereof I must hope to have your thoughts. You, that are skill'd in Caedmon's Dialect, cannot fail of being the best Interpreter of such monuments as these.

By yᵉ way—Caedmon's paraphrase (if it be not yᵉ work of a later writer) must furnish out some Notes on yʳ pentateuch. I had that Book given me (twenty years agoe) by its worthy publisher:[1] But mine wants the Title, Preface and Index. If yᵉ other printed Copies have any such furniture, an accᵗ. of 'em would be very acceptable.
Jan. 29, 1697.

(12)

SMITH TO WANLEY[2]

(Concerning ' Saxon ' manuscripts.)

I esteem it almost a piece of religion as well as civility and good manners, to answer all letters written either by friends or strangers, especially if they contain matters of learning and curiosity, which I may fairly and decently pretend to understand: which I allege that you may not give way to any ill and unjust suspicion of my having neglected or slighted your correspondence by my delay. For you must know that I have business and studye to pursue, when my health permits, which take up my thoughts and my time, as wel as you have, and am not alwais in a humour to write, when there is no necessity, tho' the trouble would be over, and the obligation satisfyed in a few minutes. Now you have explained yourself more fully about tracing out the different shapes and figurations of letters in several ages of the world, as farr as marble monuments, parchments, and medalls will reach, I shall bee very glad to assist you in the carrying of it on to that exactnes you aime at. But as to the characters used by

---

[1] Junius.

[2] Harl. MS. 3782, Art. 50; and Ellis, No. 106.

our Saxon ancestors, I meane the most antient, the Cottonian Library will afford you but little help. For tho' there is there, as everybody knowes, an excellent collection of Saxon monuments, yet farr antienter are to be met with elsewhere, particularly at Cambridge, of the guift of Archbishop Parker, and in the muniment house belonging to the Cathedral Church of Canterbury. For notwithstanding that the monks of the neighbouring monastery of S. Augustines were guilty of forging old charters for base and unworthy ends (and the like charge lyes justly against others of the same religious profession) yet I am most assured that the charters of the antient Saxon Kings of Kent, now remayning in the hands of the Deane and Chapiter as the most pretious treasure of the church, are truly genuine, and free from all suspicion of fraud: which therefore chiefly, and in the first place, ought to bee consulted. Here is a certain gentleman of quality in this place, who pretends to have the original foundation charter of the famous Monastery of Crowland . . . which I have not as yet seen, but will endeavour it, if I may, by the recommendation of a friend, obtain the favour of such an indifferent and ordinary civility. But, perchance, upon a severe examination, it may prove to bee spurious and counterfeit, like that of the Abbey of Peterborough in the Cottonian Library. . . .

So that you will conclude, that you are to expect no great matter, as to this designe, as you now explain it, from this library: but you are to seeke elsewhere; but of this you will bee the best judge upon an ocular inspection when you come next to town.

July 3, 1697.

(13)

NICOLSON TO THWAITES[1]

(Concerning Oxford editors of Old English.)

I had your kind Letter sometime agoe fro Burngeat, and this week he brought me also the Books, together wth your Supply of ye Deficiencies in my Caedmon. You will easily believe 'tis no small comfort to me to see our English Antiquities in so fair a way of being restor'd to us, in as ample a manner as any of our neighboring Nations can pretend to: And that chiefly by ye members of our own College,[2] which (I trust) will never want such Ben-

[1] MS. Rawl. D. 377.

[2] Queen's College, Oxford.

efactors to Old England as your self. I am sorry for ye trouble which your Dedication has brought upon you: and am especially concern'd at that share wch you tell me Dr Charlet had in it. I see nothing in your Epistle that can reasonably disgust the most zealous in ye services of the present Government. D^r H[1] is undoubtedly that great man you represent him to be: and tho' I doe as heartily lament the misfortune of his present circumstances as D^r Ch. himself can doe, yet I cannot but be pleas'd to see his incomparable benefaction to our Studies so gracefully acknowledg'd. Your owning me as your friend is what I shall ever think obliges me to make good that character. Amongst your Books I found Mr Rawlinson's. The pains and Charge of printing Boethius, in so generous a manner, is what (I must hope) will procure him the thanks of the present and future Ages. . . .

Dr. Hickes saies he has been hard at labour (this winter) in reviewing his Grammar, and providing for a second Edition. Is there any towardly prospect of seeing this shortly effected? I sent him my Scotch Runic Inscription,[2] as (I think) I also did to your self: But he tells me y^t he knowes not what to make of it. I suppose he has not hitherto had leisure enough to consider it.

May 7, 1698.

(14)

WANLEY TO DR. ARTHUR CHARLETT[3]

(Concerning the use of the Cottonian Library.)

Yesterday I met with Mr Chamberlain, a courteous modest, and learned Gentleman, with Mr Holmes, clerk to Mr Petit; we never saw one another before, and yet he was pleas'd to entertain so good an opinion of me at first sight, that he would needs have me dine with him, which I did; his lodgings being not two hundred yards from mine: there he entertained me very kindly, &c. From thence we went to the Exchequer, where I was introduced to Mr Le Neve, who readily shewed me Doomsday Book; the continuation of it in a lesser volume: the antient copy of them; the Pipe Roll; with the black and red Books of the Exchequer; and we promised to meet all together this night, which I have not been able to do (company coming to see me), but wrote a note to excuse myself.

[1] George Hickes.

[2] The Ruthwell Cross.

[3] Ballard MS., Vol. 16, and Ellis, No. 169.

When I returned to Sr John's, in the afternoon, the maid told me that Dr Smith had been there since I went (I had met him a little before in Westminster Hall, & saluted him, which he returned very coldly), that the Doctor was in a great rage at my being there, that he had looked into my books, & was then more angry than before: that he chid her severely for letting me into the Library, and making it common; and vowed to write to Sr John about it that night, with much more to that purpose. The maid (being my friend) advised me to go to Dr Smith and talk with him, which I did: and as I went, I considered that the D^r had three occasions to think hardly of me: one from Madam Bernard's good word of me. . . . Another that the D^r is jealous of my copying Letters from MSS. And the third is, that I did not apply myself to him in the first place, which was the greatest provocation. When I came to his lodgings, near Soho, he was gone out. I thought I must needs prevent his writing to Sr John; and therefore summoning up all the powers of rhetorick I was master of, I wrote him an humble and very submissive Letter; all his own stile; that is, I called the Library a venerable place; the Books sacred relicques of Antiquity; &c. with half a dozen tautologies; which had so good effect on him, that he came to my lodgings today . . . and left word, that I had free admittance to the Place; that he desired me to come and see him any day at 11 oclock; and seemed extremely pleased.
April 30, 1698.

(15)

WANLEY TO CHARLETT[1]

(*Difficulty of using books in the Exchequer.*)

As for Doomesday-book 'tis a most noble record; as also the Pipe-Roll of the 1st year of King John; they are both kept in the Exchequer, & I may use them about three hours in a day, but the noise and hurry is such, that I find more disturbance there than any where else; my business being not so much to transcribe a few lines from them, as to copy their several hands exactly.
May 26, 1698.

---

[1] Ballard MS., Vol. 13, and Ellis, No. 111.

(16)

NICOLSON TO THWAITES[1]

(*Subscriptions to Hickes' Thesaurus.*)

Soon after I had your Letter by yᵉ post came another from Dʳ H. with his proposals enclos'd. I wish yᵉ wealth of this country were answerable to my good will in promoting of that work. As it is, I hope to procure some small assistance towards yᵉ carrying it on. Our Bishop has promis'd to do something. Sʳ D. Fleming is also apply'd to: and I look for an encouraging Answer fro him. I have likewise hopes of soemwt from our Chapter. Upon the whole—You may depend upon yᵉ having 10 guineas sent you hence by yᵉ next return of yᵉ Carrier. If my petitions doe not bring in that Sum, yᵉ Remainder shall be furnish'd out of my own pocket. I have desir'd him to let me know what acquaintance he has in the Cathedrals at York and Durham. I can, I think, be serviceable to him at both those places. To this purpose I have requested his sending me some more Copies of his proposeals: And if you have store of 'em, I could wish you would let me have three or four by the Carrier.

Give me leave to come in with those other friends of yours that request your casting an Eye upon the Saxon Laws. You seem'd lately to promise us the result of Dʳ Hickes's pains on this subject. If he has given his papers into your hand, you are (I guess) pretty sufficiently enabled to afford us a noble Edition of those Laws: and that's what can never want a suitable Encouragement. I know not of any Helps for yᵉ supply of Sʳ H. Spelman's Deficiencies, more than what I have hinted at in yᵉ Second part of my Library; Which, by the bye, our friend Gibson (in his life of Sʳ H.) has a little misrepresented: I do not say that Mʳ Junius's Collections are yᵉ same wᵗʰ the MS in Mr. Jones's hands.

June 23, 1698.

(17)

NICOLSON TO THWAITES[1]

(*Promoting the sale of the Heptateuch.*)

Since I wrote you by Burnyeat, I have had three Copies more of Dʳ H's Proposeals: two whereof I have sent to York and Durham, and I doe hope for some good returns

Rawl. MS. D. 377.

fro thence.   Our Chapter have (capitularly) given six
Guineas: And I have yᵉ Bpˢ encouragement to hope for
as much (or near it) from him.   I shall certainly outdoe yᵉ
sum I mention'd to you in my last, I hope, considerably.
When we were discoursing this matter at Rose I took
occasion to present my Lord (in your name) wᵗʰ yᵉ A. S.
Heptateuch.   His Lordˢᵖ took it very kindly: telling me
that you were his Kinsman, and ordering me to acquaint
you yᵗ (whenever you come into yᵉ Country) he would be
thankful for as much of your company as you could spare
him.   Let me have three or four of yᵉ proposeals, by yᵉ
Carrier: if you have any stock of 'em.   I would beg, wher-
ever I have any sort of prospect of success.
July 7, 1698.

(18)

NICOLSON TO THWAITES[1]
(Concerning the delay in issuing the Thesaurus.)

I am onely concern'd to think that, if these Tables of
Coins must be added to the Septentrional Grammars, it
will be a long while before that Book is finish'd.   I am (I
assure you) already call'd on by the subscribers in this and
Neighboring Counties,[2] and I know not what Apology to
make for myself, if you do not enable me to give them
some fresh Assurances that they shall have their Books
very shortly.   'Tis a good while since you told me that the
first Alphabet was printed as far as the letter O.   This
account I presently dispers'd, and it brought in some of
the Yorkshire men; who (I find) confidently promised
themselves that, by this time, the Book would have been
in their hands.   I shall be worry'd if you help me not;
And therefore (for Charity's sake) have some compassion
upon your friend
July 10, 1699.   W. Nicolson.

(19)

DR. GEORGE HICKES TO WANLEY[3]
(Concerning the Thesaurus.)

I pray you, when you are at Cambridge, to let inquirers
know that my Book is advanced to the lv. sheet.   That its
prime cost will at least be a guiney in the lesser paper,

---

[1] MS. Rawl. D. 377, fol. 39a.

[2] Written from Edinburgh.

[3] Harl. MS. 3781, Art. 52, and Ellis, No. 118.

that its title will be *Linguarum veterum Septentrionalium Thesaurus Grammatico-Criticus et Archæologicus*, and that you do not doubt but it will answer the expectation of those learned men who have been pleased to encourage it.

I hope you'l carry your Book of Specimens with you and shew it to those gentlemen I have written to, about you and your businesse.

I advise you to keep company with none but men of learning and reputation; to let your conversation be with an air of respect and modesty to them; to behave yourself upon the place with candor, caution, and temperance; to avoid compotations; to go to bed in good time, and rise in good time; to let them see you are a man that observes houres and discipline; to make much of yourself; and want nothing that is fit for you; and dayly to pray to God, without whome nothing can be successfull and prosperous to blesse you with health, to prosper your handywork, and to give you favour and acceptance with worthy men: and I pray you to take care that your Conversation with them be civill and obliging, both for their satisfaction and your honour.

In taking the Catalogue pray put the beginning and ending of every Tract and Homily, the first and last entire sentence and the whole period, when they are not too long.

I pray God send you a good journey, and happy return to London, where we shall, God willing, meet; and after you have been some time at Cambridge, send me a short account how all things succeed with you. Direct for Dʳ Hickes, at the next house beyond the furthest lamp-post towards the feilds in King's Street, Bloomsbury. 1699.

(20)

WANLEY TO CHARLETT[1]

(Concerning Wanley's Catalogue in Hickes's Thesaurus.)

Curiosity, Sir, is a thing natural to all mankind, and more especially to all Men of Letters: and therefore it will be no wonder if I take it for granted that you desire to know what it is that keeps me here all this while, and when I design to return to Oxford. Of both which particulars I take the boldness to give you some account.

I assure you, Sir, that it is not young, idle company that detains me so much longer than I said & expected: but really the business that I came upon, which I have

[1] Ballard MSS., Vol. 13, and Ellis, No. 121.

9

found much more considerable than I could have thought for. 'Tis seven weeks since I came hither,[1] and I never wrought harder in my life for seven weeks together, than I have now done: and yet I have not finished, nor shall I be able to finish this Journey: for S[r] Thomas Bodley's bell begins to sound so loudly in my ears, that I shall not be at quiet till I'm actually in his Library.

But, Sir, you ought not to think, that there are so many Saxon MSS. in this place, as to keep a man seven weeks in barely transcribing their Titles. No, Sir, had that been all I had to do, I might have done in seven hours. But I have looked over seven score MSS. to see if I could find any Saxon words in them, and all to no purpose: . . . For other Saxon books, I have copied large pieces of them; on purpose to compare them with other books in other Libraries, that I might thereby know how they agree together. For I find we have more copies of the same book than I thought of. . . . I have further transcribed all manner of Epistles, Wills, Covenants, Notes, Charms, Verses, Catalogues, &c. that I forsee may be of use to the Book; this, & a great deal more than I say, has been one occasion of my tarrying so long. In one word, if Dr. Hickes will accept from me a Catalogue of all the Saxon MSS. that I know of in England, I will do my endeavor to restore many (hitherto anonymous Tracts) to their proper Authors: will specifie particularly whatever has been printed, & what not; with a multitude of Remarks & Observations that I have not met with in the former Edition of his book. With this Catalogue I shall annex the Specimens of the Characters of the most considerable MSS. of the Languages of the Northern Nations, as the Gothic, Francic, Langobardic, & Islandic, besides the Saxon, with specimens of MSS. in Welsh, Cornish, Scotch & Irish. . . . I shall bring with me a Scotch MS. of Receipts, an antient Lat. Eng. Dictionary containing the words of the Eastern English,[2] whereby Mr. Benson may secure many old words from being buried in the grave of everlasting oblivion.

Oct. 19, 1699.

---

[1] Cambridge.

[2] Harl. MS. 221.

(21)

GIBSON TO CHARLETT[1]

(*Criticizing Wanley's Catalogue.*)

There is one thing which I would willingly mention to you, tho' in some respects it does not become me to take notice of it. Tis Mr Wanley's Preface to the Catalogue: wch soe abounds with Anglicisms, and is wrot in a style so much different from the genius of the Latin, that I fear it will doe noe kindness to the work either at home or abroad. I would add (if Dr Wallis, a Critick were not concerned in it) that abundance of expressions seem to me to be unjust and improper. . . . Methinks every college should at least secure one for y^{eir} Libraries, which would be some assistance to the Design, tho' not soe much as might be hop'd for from so many bodies of Learned men. It is in your power and I know in your will too, to help forward the work in Oxford; as Dr Green has very kindly promis'd to doe in Cambridge, by subscribing for himself and the College as well as undertaking to solicit other heads and particular persons: soe that within ten days or a fortnight, I hope to hear a good account from there. 1700 (*circa*).

(22)

GIBSON TO CHARLETT[2]

(*Delay in issuing the Thesaurus.*)

Many questions are askt about Dr Hickes' Grammar, and abundance of foolish surmises rais'd upon its sticking in the Press soe much longer than was expected. I have been thinking, that the easiest way of answering 'em would be the publication of an Advertisement 'That nothing now remains, besides ye Catalogue and Dissertations, and that the narrowness of Junius's fund of Letters will not give leave to a quicker progress in ye work'. Sept. 17, 1700.

---

[1] Ballard MSS., Vol. 6, No. 41.

[2] Ballard MSS., Vol. 6, No. 14.

(23)

HICKES TO THWAITES[1]

(On transcribing a Greek Manuscript written in Saxon characters.)

In the printed specimen you sent me of the old Saxon hand before Alfred, fig. V, there is the beginning of the Greek-Genesis in Saxon letters. It is a sheet of Greek in Saxon Letters that I desire to have transcribed out of the MS. and none can do it right, but one who understands Saxon, as well as Greek, and therefore the trouble will fall to you. And that you may understand me better, I have here transcribed Fig. V as I would have you transcribe other the like places out of the book. . . .

Here is enough to shew you how I desire you to write the Greek in the Saxon hand viz: in the common Saxon Letters distinguishing the words, which the MS does not, and I think the Latin version need not be added. You will be best iudg wher to transcribe, and whether continually from one place or from many. . . . Perhaps half a score Lines in modern Capitalls, where it is most correct, would gratify the Learned and adorn the preface. If you think fit to transcribe as much from the Greek, add it at the end of the Greek in Saxon Letters.

Pray make what observations you can about the Power of the Saxon letters, and send them to me in the letter, in wch you inclose your sheets of transcripts. This is at present all from yours   GH.

I find by my Lord Clarendons book, y^t Burghers can work well if he will. I hope youl make him do his best in all his future work for my book.

June 23, 1702.

(24)

NICOLSON TO THOMAS BENSON[2]

(Criticizing Benson's Old English Dictionary.)

It's about three weeks since I rec'd three Copies of your Saxon Vocabulary by the Carrier. I had no Letter which accompany'd them nor any such Intimation (either before or since my Rec^t of 'em) from what hand they came: But I readily concluded that the Author was my Benefactor,

---

[1] MS. Rawl. D. 377, fol. 32a.

[2] MS. Rawl. D. 377, fol. 27.

and to him I now return my very hearty thanks. I presently sent off two of them for Scotland; where they are beginning to apply themselves, with great Vigour, to these Studies. In this particular they are fond of imitating us; and in others they think we are making all the haste we can to be like them.

On the first opening of the Book I fell in with some words said to begin with ð, which indeed are but a few, and all of 'em in Somner. I am confident ('tis a Quality wch you know, is said to be very incident to me) that there never were any such words amongst our Saxon Ancestors. In all of them, I think, the ð is mis-written for ꝥ. The first of 'em is what we Borderers, to this day call a *snude;* and so do also our friends in the antient Kingdome. In all the Rest it is easy to Observe the perverting of the Letter S.

It has been lately said that *I have no luck in Saxon;* and perhaps I am here as unfortunate as in any other Conjectures: But the Fate of many Unfortunate Lovers attends me. I am not easily to be brow beaten into a discontinuance of my Suit; even when I know I serve a coy Mistress. I wish you more successful in your Addresses than I have been.

I design, God willing, to wait on Sr Chris^r Musgrave to the next Sessions of Parliament; and am not wholly without hopes of making my personal Acknowledgements of your favour.

Oct. 2, 1701.

(25)

ELIZABETH ELSTOB TO RALPH THORESBY[1]

(*Plans of Wm. Elstob for extensive Old English publications.*)

My brother joins me in service to you. He has many things to do, if he had leisure and encouragement; King Alfred's translation of *Orosius*, he had ready for the press, and a great many materials towards the Saxon Laws, and a promise of more. He would be glad to publish Gregory's *Pastoral*, after the Homily, and being a University College man, would willingly publish all that King Alfred did. I continue my resolutions concerning the Saxon Psalms, which I set about as soon as possible after the Homily, is done.

March 22, 170⅝.

[1] Ralph Thoresby's *Correspondence*, London, 1832.

(26)

ELIZABETH ELSTOB TO THORESBY[1]

(*Concerning plans for extensive publications in Old English.*)

Your kind inquiry after my brother's health and mine, was very obliging; and we both return you our thanks. My book is at length finished, and I design to send the books on Friday by the Leeds carrier, and shall be glad to hear they are come safe to your hands. As you find it deserves, I doubt not but you will defend it against the censure of the critics. In my last I told you, I had a design upon the Psalms, but since that Mr. Wanley tells me, he is preparing the whole Bible, of which the Psalms make a part. I cannot allow myself to interfere with so excellent a person, though he has been so generous as to offer me all the assistance he can give. Having nothing else to do, I have some thoughts of publishing a set of Saxon homilies, if I can get encouragement, which I believe will be very useful; the doctrine for the most part being very orthodox, and where any errors have crept in, it may not be amiss to give some account of them. . . . My brother begs the favor of you, if you see his Grace of York, and Mr. Boulter, to let them know he designs to present them both with a book[2] by the first opportunity he meets with. This with my brother's and my humble service to yourself.

Oct. 10, 1709.

(27)

HICKES TO CHARLETT[3]

(*Concerning the Ælfric Homilies.*)[4]

If writing were not very tedious to me, I had written before to you upon recovery from my last dangerous fit to thank you for the last vol. of Leland's *Itinerary*, and for the *N. Almanack*, which obliges me now to pray God to grant you a very happy new year. I suppose you may have seen Mrs Elstob, sister of Mr Elstob, formerly fellow of your Coll. and the MSS. she hath brought to be printed at your press. The University hath acquired much

---

[1] Thoresby.

[2] Gregory's *Pastoral.*

[3] Ballard MSS., Vol. 12, No. 129, and Bliss, No. 91.

[4] Ælfric's *Homilies,* of which a few leaves were printed 1715, but never published.

reputation and honour at home and abroad, by the Saxon books printed there, as well as by those printed in Latin and Greek, and the publication of the MSS. she hath brought (the most correct I ever saw or read) will be of great advantage to the church of England against the Papists; for the honour of our predecessors the English Saxon Clergy, especially of the Episcopal Order, and the credit of our country, to which Mrs. Elstob will be counted abroad as great an ornament in her way as Madam Dacier is to France. I do not desire you to give her all encouragement, because I believe you will do it of your own accord from your natural temper to promote good and great works. But I desire you to recommend her, and her great undertaking to others, for she and it are both very worthy to be encouraged, and were I at Oxford, I should be a great solicitor for her. And had I acquaintance enough with Mr. Vice-Chancellor I had troubled him with a letter in her behalf. I will add no more but to tell you that the news of Mrs. Elstob's encouragement at the University will be very acceptable to me, because it will give her work credit here, where it shall be promoted to the utmost power by your Philo-Sax. and Philo-Goth. and most faithful, humble Servt.

Dec. 23, 1712.

(28)

HICKES TO CHARLETT[1]

(Concerning Northern studies at home and abroad.)

Mr. Elstob and his sister set out tomorrow for Oxford, I renew my hearty request to you to promote subscriptions to her most useful book. Had I the honour of so much acquaintance wth M——— to write to him, I would entreat him also to be one of her subscribers, for the reputation of the Oxford subscriptions will procure many here and in Cambridge. And that was the method I took of getting subscriptions to my own book. Had it not been for the fire at Mr Boyers 3 nights after that which had like to have burnt us, you had seen a very handsome commendation in a short time of the University of Oxford for encouraging and promoting the old Septentrional Learning by Mr. (F———?) of the Inner Temple whose book among many others was burnt. I pray you to give my very faithful and humble service to the Provost of Queen's and

[1] Ballard MSS., Vol. 12, No. 130.

tell him I hope yt he and you will set up each of you some young men to study the Septentrional Languages wᶜʰ now they are studying ding-dong in several parts of Germany, since my book got among them.

Feb. 24, 17$\frac{1}{8}\frac{2}{8}$.

(29)

HICKES TO CHARLETT[1]

(Sale of Thesaurus.)

I give you all hearty thanks for the great and seasonable kindness you have done me in getting 5 copies of my *Thesaurus* taken off my hands, and I pray you to give my respective thanks and acknowledgements to those very kind and obliging gentlemen, who are my friends so much, as to take them for their College Libraries. Were I able, I would go with the remainder of my copies to Paris, where they are much wanted. Monsr. L'Abbé Gautier made me hope, that he would get them put into all the libraries of the French Monasteries, but he hath failed me, and I wrote almost 3 months ago to Sir Andrew Fountain at Paris, who sent me word that they wanted my book there, but I have not heard from him. I shall in a little time write again to you.

1713.

(30)

HICKES TO CHARLETT[2]

(Sale of Thesaurus.)

By this time I hope you have received the five books. They are indeed of the lesser paper; but may very well pass for those of the greater, if not compared together. The public Libraries throughout the nation, except the Bodleian, have no other. Those in the greater having been sold for the libraries of princes, and the private libraries of great men, and others who had a mind to them. Of the six which I told Mr Bishop I had in the great paper, one is reserved for my Lord Treasurer, another for the Spanish Embassador at his return, to be put in the Escurial Library, a third I reserve for myself; but if any of your friends will have any of the other three at the price viz.,

---

[1] Bliss, No. 98.

[2] Bliss, No. 99.

five guineas, they may. When Palthenius,[1] the learned German saw the book in the less paper, he cried out with admiration to Mr Thwaites, who shewed it him, *Per Deum, nihil Gallia sub auspiciis Ludovici Magni magnificentius aut augustius edidit.*

I desired Mr Bishop to tell you, that the common price of my book in the lesser paper was three guineas; but I never set any price to Colleges or other Societies. . . . As for Magdalen Hall, I will present them with a copy of my book, but will take it as a particular respect from Dr. Blechinton, if he pleases to take one copy for the Library of Worcester College. You will have as many copies of the small paper, at three guineas, the common price, as you shall give order for. I pray you to give my most humble thanks and acknowledgements to the Principal of Brasenose, Warden of Wadham, Provost of Oriel, and Master of Pembroke, for their kindness to me in taking copies of my book; and to all others who have so much kindness for me, and assure them I shall ever think myself obliged to them. . . .

Dear Sir, I pray God reward you for your kindness to me in this affair of my book, of which I had had no copies now to put off, had it not been for the late war.

Dec. 29, 1713.

(31)

WILLIAM BISHOP TO CHARLETT[2]

(*Ælfric's Homilies.*)

Being ys day wᵗʰ Mrs Elstob, I find by Her yᵗ she has great encouragemᵗ & many subscribers at Cambridge & little countenance & few subscribers in Oxford that she prints the Saxon Homilies there. I can but wonder at it, not doubting but ye colleges would all subscribe for their libraries. I should be glad to know the reason so few subscribe at Oxford. I believe notwithstanding yt she will not want subscribers she printing but a few. Good Dʳ Hickes has often declared to me it was as well done as could be desired or expected; as well done as if He had undertaken it.

Feb. 20, 171⅚.

---

[1] Johann Philip Palthen (1672-1710), who in 1698 made a journey to Oxford to see the Junian manuscripts.

[2] Ballard MSS., Vol. 32, No. 12.

(32)

GIBSON TO CHARLETT[1]

(*Concerning the establishment of a Saxon lecture at Oxford.*)

I had heard nothing of an established Saxon Lecture, till I received your letter, nor do I yet know who the founder is, or what the Salary. When the present Bishop of Derry[2] was Almoner, I have heard him speak of applying the allowance made by the late Bp. of Worcester to one or more Professors of the Oriental Languages, to a Saxon lecture, but I do not remember that he ever told me the thing was settled. My knowledge in that way is almost gone, thro' disuse; but yet I have a great desire, before I die, to make the *Saxon Chronicle* a complete work; by additions which may be had from other Manuscripts, and by reducing every piece of History whatever that has been originally written in Saxon, and maybe determined to a certain year or near it, with one body of *Saxon Annals;* with proper distinction to shew from whence every thing is taken. There are, I take it, many Saxon pieces which, tho' never part of any formal Book of Annals, are of undoubted authority, as truly historical as the Annals themselves. . . .

The way that Mr. Hearne and Mr Hall are got into, of publishing our English historians which have not been published before, ought to be greatly encouraged; but why so few copies to be printed of every book? Every person who is possessed of one of those books, will naturally reckon that he has a greater treasure because the copies are few; but certainly the end of printing was to multiply copies, and to spread them into many more hands, and to make learning more accessible than it was before. The notion of greater value should give way to greater use. Jan. 2, 17$\frac{19}{20}$.

(33)

DR. JOHN THORPE TO THOMAS HEARNE[3]

(*Trouble in printing the Textus Roffensis.*)

Mr Barrell told me, that being lately with the Dean of Rochester, the Dean[4] seemed apprehensive that publishing the *Textus* would make the Rochester MS. less valuable,

---

[1] Ballard MSS., Vol. 6, No. 83; and Bliss, No. 131.

[2] Wm. Nicolson.   [3] Bliss, No. 134.   [4] Dr. Prat.

and spoke as if he designed to enter a claim at Stationers'
Hall in order to secure to the Dean and Chapter their
property in the Copy. To obviate which Mr Barrell wrote
yesterday to the Dean, and acquainted him that it was the
opinion of himself, and other Prebendaries, that printing
the *Textus* would no ways lessen the value of their MS.
that they were rather desirous that it might come abroad,
and as correct and compleat as possible; and that therefore
they hoped he would desist from entering any claim as he
proposed, and would give leave (if you desired it) either
to collate your Edition[1] with the MS. or to supply you
with anything out of it that you should have occassion for.
May 17, 1720.

[1] Hearne edited the *Textus Roffensis* at Oxford, 1720, from the MS.
of Sir Edward Dering.

APPENDIX II

(a)

A SAXON TREATISE CONCERNING THE OLD AND NEW TESTAMENT, &c.

By William L'Isle, 1623.

Table of Contents to the Preface.

Extracts from the Preface.

To the Readers.

1. That I put not out anything rashly in print, especially
of this kinde, and in this Age so ready to controll;
and that I may do somewhat more than translate;
which is but a painfull office vnder another man; I
thought meet thus to exercise my Pen first by way
of Preface. Then take ye this notice (discreet and
gentle Readers) that here I offer vnto your view
(as the title shewes) an ancient monument of the
Church of *England.* If I should say no more, that
name onely implieth reason enough to shew it
worthy preseruation among vs, euen in this old
garbe and character now almost forgotten: but
that it perish not altogether, as it was like, by this
all-deuouring time, such knowledge thereof, as
God hath giuen me, I shall gladly impart; and try
by this little, before I trust much: entending ere
long, if this be well accepted, to publish more of
the same kind. . . .

2. I regard not the enuious or malignant humour of
some; who when they see any man haue skill neuer
so little in thing vncommon, because they know it
not themselues, are ready, if he haue any other
good parts, to blemish them all with a by-word of
that one: and would for this haue him counted but
a Saxon (which they laugh at, as vaine) though he
knew moreouer the learneder tongue and Arts as
well as they. Howsoeuer it deserues (I grant) no
great commendation, I am sure it is far from a
fault, to know these ouer-aged and outworne dialects, especially of our owne tongue, which I desire
to aduance; and some further good vse I trust to
make and shew you thereof ere I haue done. . . .

4. Lo here in this field of learning, this orchard of the
old English Church, haue I set my selfe on worke,
where though I plant not a new, I may saue at
least a good old tree or two, that were like to be
lost: now, for a triall, this remnant of the learned
Ælfrikes writing; as I meane to doe ere long (if it
may be accepted) a part of the Bible which our
Saxon Ancestors left us in their owne tongue. . . .

8. The Saxons a people most deuout (as by the Monasteries and Churches they built appeares) having
in our Libraries so goodly monuments of reuerend

antiquitie, diuine handwritings, in so faire and large character, that a man running may read them; doe not make them knowne to the world; but let them lie still like a treasure hid, to no vse; and euen till they be almost forgotten of our selues. . . .

9. The due consideration hereof first stirred-vp in me an earnest desire to know what learning lay hid in this old English tongue: for which I found out this vneasie way, first to acquaint myselfe a little with the Dutch both high and low; the one by originall, the other by commerce allied: then to read awhile for recreation all the old English I could find, poetry or prose, of what matter soeuer. And diuers good bookes of this kinde I got, that were neuer yet published in print; which euer the more ancient they were, I perceived came neerer the Saxon: But the Saxon, (as a bird, flying in the aire farther and farther, seemes lesse and lesse;) the older it was, became harder to bee vnderstood. At length I lighted on *Virgil* Scotished by the Reuerend *Gawin Dowglas* Bishop of *Dunkell*, and vncle to the Earle of *Angus;* the best translation of that Poet that euer I read: And though I found that dialect more hard than any of the former (as neerer the Saxon, because farther from the Norman) yet with helpe of the Latine I made shift to vnderstand it, and read the booke more than once from the beginning to the end. Wherby I must confesse I got more knowledge of that I sought than by any of the other. For as at the Saxon Inuasion many of the Britans, so at the Norman many of the Saxons fled into Scotland, preseruing in that Realme vnconquered, as the line Royall, so also the language, better than the Inhabitants here, vnder conquerors law and custome, were able. Next then I read the decalogue &c. set out by *Fraerus*[1] in common character, and so prepared came to the proper Saxon; which differeth but in seuen or eight letters from the Pica Roman; and therein reading certaine Sermons, and the foure Euangelists set out and Englished by Mr *Fox*, so increased my skill, that at length (I thank God) I found my selfe able (as it were to swimme without bladders) to vnderstond the vn-

---

[1] Marq. Freheri *Decalogi, Orationes, Symboli,* 1610.

translated fragments of the tongue scattered in
Master *Cambden* and others, by him some, and
some by Sir *Henry Savill* set forth: so also those
in Tho: of *Walsingham*, *Caius*, and *Lambard;* with
certaine old charters that I met with among the
Kings Records, and in the Coucher-bookes of
Monasteries; Yet still ventring not far from the
shore. At last waxing more able through vse, I
tooke heart to put forth and diue into the deep
among the meere Saxon monuments of my worthily
respected kinsman Sir *H. Spelman*, my honorable
friend Sir *Rob. Cotton* & of our Libraries in Cambridge. So far about went I for want of a guide,
who now (thanks be to God) am able to lead
others a neerer way. . . .

15. But this good ordinance of preseruing Standard-
Bibles in our Cathedral Churches or in the Kings
Chappell, had it continued, we might haue shewed
now the whole booke of God in Saxon, . . .
whereof a part hath beene set forth already by
good master *Fox*, and (by the grace of God) I
meane ere long to let the world know what is more
remaining; as more I haue seene both in our Vni-
uersitie Libraries, and that of Sir *Robert Cotton*.

17. We lacke but a Grammar which our Saxon Ancestors
neglected not, as appeares by that of this *Ælfricus*
yet extant in many faire-written copies. The like
if we had for the language of our time, it would
giue vs occassion either in wording or sentensing,
the principall parts thereof, to looke backe a little
into this outworne dialect of our forebeers; which
England hath kept best in writing, *Scotland* in
speech. I speake not, I wish not this to the end
we should againe call this old garbe into vse; but to
hold where we are without borrowing when we need
not: and that whoso will, may the more easily
come to the understanding of these so venerable
handwritings and monuments of our owne antiquity: without which we can neither know well
our lawes, nor our Histories, nor our owne names,
nor the names of places and bound-markes of our
Country. . . .

18. Why should we not bear . . . affection to the mean
and rude beginnings of our tongue not withstand-
ing the perfection it is now come to. Thankes be
to God that he that conquered the Land could

not so conquer the Language; . . . and even at this day we all speake and write it after a sort; yea are able (some) to vnderstand it, as it was then spoken and written. If you aske mee to what purpose, I answer, first to know and make knowne to the world, that, howsoeuer the Scripture in vulgar hath beene since debarred; yet our Saxon Ancestors had both this and other bookes of Diuinity in the mother tongue; and to note in what sort it was then translated. Secondly, the memory and knowledge thereof serues well to finde out, when need is, the Etymologies and roots of our words and names now used: which many not knowing, doe much mistake. . . . A third use of this knowledge is, to vnderstand the right meaning of our old lawes, which often give light to the new: And herein Master *Lambert*[1] hath taken good paines; yet affecting too much the analogicall Latine, he leaues many times vntold the true sense of our Saxon. A fourth vse thereof is that we may be able to declare vnto all men, whom it concernes, the true meaning of their titles, charters, priuiledges, territories and precincts. . . . The sixt and last vse that I will now speake of (for I haue no time for all) is to decide controuersies often arising among our Heraulds and Antiquaries; as what meanes . . . an Alderman, a Thane, a Bydel, a Sherife, . . . &c not all so necessary as the rest; yet euen for these also, and much more for the other, I hold the knowledge of this old English, and any good matter of humanity therein written, but diuinity above all, worthy to be preserued. . . . What Englishman of vnderstanding is there, but may be delighted to see, the prety shifts our tongue made with her owne store, in all parts of learning, when they scorned to borrow words of another? Albeeit now sithence wee haue taken that liberty which our neighbours doe; and to requite them more then for need, our language is improued above all others now spoken by any nation, and became the fairest, the nimblest, the fullest; most apt to vary the phrase, most ready to receiue good composition, most adorned with sweet words and sentences, with witty quips and ouer-ruling Prou-

[1] William Lambarde.

erbes: yea able to expresse any conceit whatsoeuer
with great dexterity; waighty in weighty matters,
merry in merry, braue in braue. . . . But sure
to neglect the beginnings of such an excellent
tongue, will bring vpon vs the foule disgrace not
onely of ignorance . . . but of extreme ingratitude towards our famous ancestors, who left vs
so many, so goodly monuments in their old Dialect recorded.

(*b*)

AN ENGLISH-SAXON HOMILY ON THE BIRTH-DAY OF ST. GREGORY

By Elizabeth Elstob, 1709

Extracts from the Preface.

For the Satisfaction of more candid Readers, I shall
give some short Account of the Motives that urged me to
this Undertaking, and of the Performance it self.

Having accidentally met with a Specimen of K. Alfred's
Version of *Orosius* into Saxon, design'd to be published by
a near Relation and Friend,[1] I was very desirous to understand it, and having gain'd the Alphabet, I found it so
easy, and in it so much of the grounds of our present Language, and of a more particular Agreement with some
Words which I had heard when very young in the North
as drew me in to be more inquisitive after Books written in
that Language. With this, the Kind Encourager of my
Studies being very well pleased, recommended to me the
Saxon Heptateuch, most accurately published by Mr.
Thwaites. The Matter of that Book being well known and
familiar to me, made the reading of it very easy and agreeable: and led me on to the reading of several other Treatises,
and to divert my self in taking Transcripts from such ancient Manuscripts as I could meet with. Among these was
one I made of the *Athanasian Creed*, which the Great In-
staurator of Northern Literature[2] was pleased to accept from
me: and to think not unworthy of being publish'd with
the *Conspectus* or account in Latin, which the learned Mr.
Wotton has given us of his ample and learned *Thesaurus
Linguarum Vett. Septentrionalium*. This great patron of
the Septentrional Studies, hath ever since presevered to

[1] William Elstob.

[2] Dr. George Hickes.

10

encourage my Proceeding in them, and to urge me that by publishing somewhat in Saxon, I would invite the Ladies to be acquainted with the Language of their Predecessors, and the Original of their Mother Tongue. Particularly he recommended to me the Publication of this *Homily*. And here I cannot but observe, how great an Argument Women have, for engaging in Learning, even Saxon Learning, from so great an Authority. . . .

But to come to the *Homily* upon St. Gregory. When I had read it over, and transcribed it, I made no long Dispute of it, whether or no I shou'd make it English. The Importance of the History, and the happy Circumstances of our Conversion, gave me no small Pleasure, in attending upon that Performance. This, I confess, I have not done with any great Elegance, according to the Genius of our present Idiom; having chosen rather to use such English as wou'd be both intelligible and best express the Saxon; that, as near as possible, both the Saxon and the English might be discerned to be of the same kindred and affinity: and the Reader be more readily enabled and encouraged to know the one by the other; which end I immagine would not be so well answer'd by a Translation more polite and elaborate. In following the course of the *Homily*, I added such Notes as I thought wou'd be some way or other useful, or at least diverting. I am sensible, in such a Variety, there will be different Occasion of Censure; and that things will either please or displease, according to the different Humor and Relish of the several Readers.

But to return to the *Homily* on St. Gregory. It is printed from a Transcript I had made of it from one made by Dr. Hopkins, I believe out of the Cottonian Book, Vitellius D. 17. . . . The *Homily* was one of those prepared by Ælfrick, to be used in the English Saxon Church; and is the ninth in the second of those two Volumes, which contained a course of Sermons, and were to be recited to the People, in the course of one or two years, as shou'd be judged most fit. He stiles himself Ælfrick, Monk, and Priest, and dedicates both Volumes to Sigeric, Archbishop of Canterbury, whose Successor he was in that See. He professes, that for the Prevention of Heresie and the Doctrine of Deceivers, he had in these Sermons chiefly followed the Authority of the ancient Fathers, viz. St. Augustine of Hippo, St. Jerom, Bede and St. Gregory &c. The reason of his translating these Books out of Latin into English, was not, as he himself declares, out of Presumption of any great Learning; but because he saw and observed, much error in many English Books; which the unlearned, out of their Simplicity, took for great Wisdom. That it grieved him, that they knew not and had not, the Gospel Learning in their Writings; save such alone as understood Latin, and such as cou'd have those Books which K. Ælfred wisely translated out of Latin into English. . . . The Transcript of this *Homily* I compared with that antient Parchment *Book of Homilies* in the Bodleian Library amongst Junius' Books N.E.F. 4. being the second of those Volumes that had formerly belong'd to the Hattonian Library, an Account of which we have in that most elaborate Catalogue of Saxon Manuscripts by Mr Wanley, which makes the second Volume of Dr. Hickes *Thesaurus*, p. 43. I had access to this Book by the singular Courtesy of Dr. Hudson, a Person of so much Learning; that, as he needs not envy it in any other, so has he that generous Quality to be found only in those great and generous minds that are inform'd with a truly Scholar-like Genius; of not discouraging Learning, even in our Sex.

Having given an Account of the Homilist, some will expect, somewhat shou'd be said of the Translator. I have been askt the Question, more than once, whether this Performance was all my own? How properly such a Question may be ask'd by those who know with whom I live, I shall not dispute: But since some there are who may have a Curiosity to know the same thing, who yet suspect the Decency of such a Question; that they may be under no Uneasiness on this account, they may be pleased to understand that I have a kind Brother,[1] who is always ready to assist and encourage me in my Studies. I might say much of my Obligations on this account: would he permit me to express myself at large on that Subject. But as I think it no shame to me to take any Advice where it may be so easily obtain'd: so I should think it unpardonable to be guilty of such a Silence, as might make me seem averse to all Acknowledgement.

I have little more to add, than my Thanks to all my Encouragers, which have far exceeded the Number I cou'd have expected to a first Attempt; the greatest Part whereof have done me a great deal of Honour by the Countenance both of their Quality and Learning, and to all I am one way or other obliged for their kindness and esteem. I am very glad to find so many of the Ladies, and those, several of them, of the best Rank; favouring these Endeavours of a Beginner, and one of their Sex.

[1] William Elstob.

(c)

THE RUDIMENTS OF GRAMMAR FOR THE ENGLISH SAXON TONGUE, ETC.

By Elizabeth Elstob, 1715

Dedication to the Grammar.

To Her Royal Highness the Princess of Wales.

Madam: This small Treatise, which the Author once hoped to have the Honour of dedicating to Her Royal Highness the Princess Sophia, a Lady endowed with all Princely Accomplishments, and particularly a most Bounteous Patroness of Letters, begs leave now most humbly to offer itself to Your Royal Highness's gracious Acceptance, who so undoubtedly inherit all the Royal and Illustrious Qualities of that Great Lady.

Madam: it addresses itself to Your Royal Highness, congratulating Your Auspicious Arrival into England, in a Language which bears a name that is common both to the German and English Nations, the Saxon. This will not, I presume, make it a less agreeable Present to Your Royal Highness, in whose Royal Offspring the Saxon Line is to be continued, with encrease of all Princely and Heroick Virtues. If this may seem too much a Trifle, to deserve Admittance to Your Royal Highness, it being a Treatise of Grammar, Your Royal Highness will be pleased to remember, that it hath not only been thought worthy of their Protection, but even to employ the Pens of some great Emperors and Kings. Julius Caesar writ three Books, *de Analogia*, and the Emperor Charlemaign, from whom so many Renowned Princes are descended, composed a Grammar for his own Language, the ancient Francick; which is the Mother of the present German, and of near Alliance with the *Anglo-Saxon*, all of them confessing their Original from the Goths.

Hoping it might yield some kind of Diversion to Your Royal Highness, I have here and there interspersed some Instances, of German, Francick, and Gothick Words, whereby that Affinity is declared. I am the more in hopes of Your Royal Highness's kind Aspect upon this little Work, after the Precedent of such Great and Royal Examples, when I understand that His Majesty, Your Royal Father, Our most gracious Sovereign, who is a great Judge and Promoter of all good Learning, doth in a more particular manner recommend the cultivating the Study of the German Antiquities; in order to the right Understanding and Illustration of which, the Knowledge of the English-Saxon Language and Antiquities, is so very necessary. I have but one thing more to add, that this Present, worthless as it is, is the humble Tribute of a Female, the First, I imagin, of the kind that hath been offer'd to Your Royal Highness: Such as it is, it desires with all Submission, to be received into Your Royal Highness's Favourable Protection, together with the Author, who with most hearty Prayers for Your Royal Highness, and Your whole Royal House, begs leave to subscribe herself.

May it please Your Royal Highness,

Your Royal Highness's

most Dutiful and most

Obedient Humble Servant,

Elizabeth Elstob.

Selections from the Preface.

To the Reverend Dr. Hickes.

Sir, Soon after the Publication of the *Homily on St. Gregory*, I was engaged by the Importunity of my Friends, to make a Visit to Canterbury, as well to enjoy the Conversation of my Friends and Relations there, as for that Benefit which I hoped to receive from Change of Air, and freer Breathing, which is the usual Expectation of those, who are used to a sedentary Life and Confinement in the great City, and which renderes such an Excursion now and then Excusable. In this Recess, among the many Compliments and kind Expressions, which their favourable Acceptance of my first Attempt in Saxon had obtain'd for me from the Ladies, I was more particularly gratified, with the new Friendship and Conversation of a young Lady, whose Ingenuity and Love of Learning is well known and esteem'd, not only in that Place, but by yourself: and which so far endeared itself to me, by her promise that she wou'd learn the Saxon Tongue, and do me the Honour to be my Scholar, as to make me think of composing an English Grammar of that Language for her use. That Ladies Fortune hath so disposed of her since that time, and hath placed her at so great distance, as that we have no Opportunity of treating farther on this Matter, either by Discourse or Correspondence. However though a Work of a larger Extent,[1] and which hath amply experienced your Encouragement, did for some time make me lay aside this Design, yet I did not wholly reject it. For

---

[1] Ælfric's *Homilies.*

having re-assumed this Task and accomplish'd it in such manner as I was able, I now send it to you, for your Correction and that Stamp of Authority, it must needs receive from a Person of such perfect and exact Judgement in these Matters, in order to make it current, and worthy of Reception from the Publick. Indeed I might well have spared myself the labour of such an Attempt, after the elaborate Work of your rich and learned *Thesaurus*, and the ingenius Compendium of it by Mr Thwaites, but considering the pleasure I myself had reaped from the Knowledge I have gained from this Original of our Mother Tongue, and that others of my own Sex, might be capable of the same Satisfaction: I resolv'd to give them the Rudiments of that Language in an English Dress. However not till I had communicated to you my Design for your Advice, and had receiv'd your repeated Exhortation, and Encouragement to the Undertaking.

The Method I have used is neither entirely new, out of a Fondness and Affectation of Novelty; nor exactly the same with what has been in use in teaching the learned Languages. I have retained the old Division of the Parts of Speech, nor have I rejected the other common Terms of Grammar; I have only endeavour'd to explain them in such a manner, as to hope they may be competently understood by those whose Education, hath not allow'd them an Acquaintance with the Grammars of other Languages. There is one Addition to what yourself and Mr Thwaites have done on this Subject, for which you will, I immagine, readily pardon me: I have given most, if not all the Grammatical Terms in true old Saxon, from Ælfricks Translation of Priscian, to shew the polite Men of our Age, that the Language of their Forefathers is neither so barren nor barbarous as they affirm, with equal Ignorance and Boldness. . . . These Gentlemans ill Treatment of our Mother Tongue[1] has led me into a Stile not so agreeable to the Mildness of our Sex, or the usual manner of my Behaviour, to Persons of your Character; but the Love and Honour of one's Country, hath in all Ages been acknowledg'd such a Virtue, as hath admitted of a Zeal even somewhat extravagant. . . . The Justness and Propriety of the Language of any Nation, hath been always rightly esteem'd a great Ornament and Test of the good Sense of such a Nation, and consequently to arraign the good Sense or Language of any Nation, is to cast upon it a great Reproach. Even private Men are most jealous, of

---

[1] Cf. the Swift-Temple-Wotton controversy.

any Wound, that can be given them in their intellectual
Accomplishments, which they are less able to endure, than
Poverty itself or any other kind of Disgrace. . . . But
it is very remarkable how Ignorance will make Men bold,
and presume to declare that unnecessary which they will
not be at pains to render useful. . . . It had been well
if those wise Grammarians had understood this Character,
who have taken upon them to teach our Ladies and young
Gentlemen, the whole System of an English Education:
they had not incurr'd those Self-contradictions of which
they are guilty; they had not mention'd your incomparable
Treasury of Northern Literature in so cold and negligent
a manner, as betrays too much of an invidious Pedantry:
But in those Terms of Veneration and Applause which are
your just Tribute, not only from the Learned of your own
Countrey, but of most of the other Northern Nations,
whether more or less Polite: Who would any of them
glory'd in having you their Native, who have done so much
Honour to the Original of almost all the Languages in
Europe. But it seems you are not of so much Credit with
these Gentlemen, who question your Authority, and have
given a very visable Proof of their Ingenuity in an Instance
which plainly discovers, that they cannot believe their
own Eyes. 'The Saxons, say they, if we may credit Dr.
Hickes, had various Terminations to their Words, at least
two in every Substantive singular, whereas we have no
Word now in use, except the personal Names that has so.
Thus Dr. Hickes has made six several Declensions of the
Saxon Names: He gives them three Numbers; a Singular,
Dual, and Plural: We have no Dual Number, except perhaps in 'Both.' . . . I would aske these Gentlemen,
and why not credit Dr. Hickes? Is he not as much to be
believ'd as those Gentlemen. . . . Did he make those six
Declensions? or rather, did he not find them in the Language, and take so much pains to teach others to distinguish
them, who have Modesty enough to be taught? . . . Yet
if these Gentlemen will not credit Dr Hickes, the Saxon
Writings might give them full Satisfaction. The Gospels,
the Psalms, and a great part of the Bible are in Saxon, so
are the Laws and Ecclesiastical Canons, and Charters of
most of our Saxon Kings; these one wou'd think might
deserve their Credit. But they have not had Learning or
Industry enough to fit them for such Acquaintance and
are forc'd therefor, to take up their Refuge with those
Triflers, whose only Pretence to Wit is to despise their
Betters. This Censure will not, I imagine, be thought

harsh, by any candid Reader, since their own Discovery
has sufficiently declared their Ignorance; and their Boldness, to determine things whereof they are so ignorant,
has so justly fix'd upon them the Charge of Impudence.
For otherwise they must needs have been ashamed to
proceed in manner following.

'We might give you various Instances more of the
essential difference between the old Saxon and modern
English Tongue, but these must satisfy any reasonable
Man that it is so great that the Saxon can be no Rule to
us; and that to understand ours, there is no need of knowing the Saxon: and tho' Dr. Hickes must be allow'd to have
been a very curious Enquirer into those obsolete Tongues,
now out of use, and containing nothing valuable, yet it
does by no means follow (as is plain from what has been
said) that we are obliged to derive the Sense, Construction, or Nature of our present Language from his Discoveries.'

What they say, that it cannot be a Rule to them, is
true; for nothing can be a Rule of Direction to any Man,
the use whereof he does not understand; but if to understand the Original and Etymology of the Words of any
Language be needful towards knowing the Propriety of
any Language, a thing which I have never heard hath
yet been denied, then do these Gentlemen stand self-
condemned. . . . Their great condescension to Dr.
Hickes in allowing him to have been a curious Inquirer
into those obsolete Tongues, now out of use, and containing nothing valuable in them, is a Compliment for which
I believe you, Sir, will give me leave to assure them, that
he is not at all obliged; since if it signifies anything, it im-
ports, no less than that he has employ'd a great deal of
Time and a great deal of Pains, to little Purpose. But we
must at least borrow so much Assurance from them, as to
tell them, that your Friends, who consist of the most
learned Sort of your own Country-men, and of Foreigners,
do not think those Tongues so obsolete and out of use,
whose Significancy is so apparent in Etymology; nor do
they think those Men competent Judges to declare, whether
there be any thing contain'd in them valuable or not, who
have made it clear, that they know not what is contain'd
in them. They wou'd rather assure them, that our greatest
Divines and Lawyers, and Historians are of another
Opinion, they wou'd advise them to consult our Libraries,
those of the two Universities, the Cottonian, and my
Lord Treasurer's to study your whole *Thesaurus*, par-

ticularly your *Dissertatio Epistolaris,* to look into Mr
Wanleys large and accurate *Catalogue of Saxon Manuscripts,* and so with Modesty gain a Title to the Applause of having confest their former Ignorance, and re-
forming their Judgement. I believe I may farther take
leave to assure them, that the Doctor is as little concerned
for their Inference, which they think so plain from what
has been said, that they are not obliged to derive the
Sense, Construction, or Nature of our present Language
from his Discoveries. He desires them not to derive the
Sense and Construction of which they speak, in any other
manner, than that in which the Nature of the things
themselves make them appear, and so far as they are his
Discoveries only, intrudes them on no man. He is very
willing they should be let alone by those, who have not
Skill to use them to their own Advantage, and with Grat-
itude.

But to leave these Pedagogues to huff and swagger in
the heighth of all their Arrogance I cannot but think it a
great Pity, that in our Considerations, for Refinement of
the English Tongue, so little Regard is had to Antiquity,
and the Original of our present Language, which is the
Saxon.   .   .   .

The want of knowing the Northern Languages, has
occasion'd an unkind Prejudice towards them: which some
have introduc'd out of Rashness, others have taken upon
Tradition. As if those Languages were made up of nothing
else but Monosyllables, and harsh sounding Consonants;
than which nothing can be a greater Mistake. I can speak
for the Saxon, Gothick, and Francick, or old Teutonick:
which for aptness of compounded, and well sounding
words and variety of Numbers, are by those learned men
that understand them, thought scarce inferior to the
Greek itself. I never cou'd find myself shocked with the
Harshness of those Languages, which grates so much in
the Ears of those that never heard them. I never per-
ceiv'd in the consonants any Harshness but such as was
necessary to afford Strength, like Bones in a human Body,
which yield it Firmness and Support. So that the worst
that can be said on this occasion of our Forefathers is, that
they spoke as they fought, like men.   .   .   .

To conclude: if this Preface is writ in a Stile, that
may be thought somewhat rough and too severe, it is not
out of any natural Inclination to take up a Quarrel, but to
do some Justice to the Study of Antiquities, and even of
our own Language itself, against the severe Censurers of

both. If I am mistaken herein, I beg Pardon. . . . I confess I thought it would be to little purpose to write an English Saxon Grammar, if there was nothing of Worth in that Language to invite any one to the study of it. . . .

Sir, I once more heartily beg your Pardon for giving you so much trouble, and beg leave to give you my Thanks for the great Assistance I have receiv'd in the Saxon Studies from your learned Works, and Conversation; and in particular for your favourable Recommendation of my Endeavours, in a farther cultivating those Studies, who with sincere Wishes for your good Health and all imaginable Respect for a Person of your Worth and Learning, am   Sir, Your Most Obliged,
                              Humble Servant,
                              Elizabeth Elstob.

Day.

IC Ine mıd ʒoðer ʒyƀe perʦreoxna cý-
nınʒ.mıd ʒeþeahʦ ⁊ mıð læne cennoðer
mınner ƿæðerı.⁊ heoðer mıner bırceoper.
⁊ coꝛcenꝑolðer mıner bırceoper. ⁊ mıð
eallum mınum ealðoꝛmannum. ⁊ þam ýlðeſʦan pı-
ʦan mınꝛe þeoðe. ⁊ eıc mýcelne ꝛomnunʒe ʒoðer
þeoꝑena. þær ſmeaʒenðe be ðæꝛe hæle unꝛa ꝛaꝑla. ⁊
be ðam ſʦaþole uꝛer ꝛıcer. þ nýhʦ æꝛ.⁊ nýhʦe cý-
neðǫm ıſ.þuꝛh uꝛe ƀolc ʒeƀærʦenoðe. ⁊ ʒeʦꝛým-
með ꝑæꝛon. þ nænıʒ ealðoꝛmanna. ne uſ unðeꝛʒe-
þeoðenðꝛa. æƀʦeꝛ ðæm ꝑæꝛe aꝑenðenðe þær uꝛe
ðomıꝛ;

Be ʒoðer þeoꝑena ꝛeʒole;

Æꝛerʦ ꝑe bebeoðæþ. þ ʒoðer þeoꝑar hıoꝛa ꝛýhʦ
ꝛeʒole ʒýman. ⁊ on nýhʦ healðan; Æƀʦeꝛ þam ꝑe
beoðæþ. þ ealler ƀolcer * æ. ⁊ ðomar þuꝛ ꝛýnð ʒe-
healðene;

(marginal: teꝛ· ... ·uꝛ· ƀue·)

Be cılðum;

Cılð bınnan þꝛýʦʦıʒum nıhʦa ſý ʒeƀulꝑað.
ʒıƀ hıʦ ſꝑa ne ſý. xxx. ꝛcıllınʒer ʒebeʦe; Gıƀ hıð
bonnaꝛıſ ... hurʦan ...luhʦe. ʦebeʦe he hıʦ mıð

Lambarde, *Archaionomia*, 1568.

APPENDIX III

(a)

A BRIEF ACCOUNT OF THE USE OF ANGLO-SAXON TYPES

The use of Anglo-Saxon types for printing Old English dates from 1566, and the practice continued well into the nineteenth century.[1] The Anglo-Saxons themselves may have been ignorant of letters when they came into England, and there is, of course, no such thing as a distinctive Anglo-Saxon 'character'. The Old English manuscripts were written in a hand adapted from the Roman minuscule used by the Irish monks. The last stage of this hand, which Thomas Astle termed 'Elegant Saxon',[2] flourished from the early tenth century to the Norman Conquest. Among Old English manuscripts of this period were Ælfric's *Homilies*, the *Pentateuch*,[3] and Cædmon's *Paraphrase of the Gospels*;[4] since these were among the earliest specimens of the language to be printed, these manuscripts undoubtedly furnished the model for Anglo-Saxon types.

John Day was the first printer to use Anglo-Saxon types; these were of brass, cast at the expense of Archbishop Parker, for the printing of *A Testimonie of Antiquitie*, 1566. They exhibit what is called a full Anglo-Saxon letter. The body of the type was English, a little less than Great Primer; of the capitals, eight, including two diphthongs, were 'Saxon', the rest being ordinary Roman;

[1] The vacillation of Thorpe in the use of Anglo-Saxon types illustrate their decline in the nineteenth century. He prints his *Cædmon*, 1832; *Ancient Laws*, 1840; *Codex Exoniensis*, 1842; in Anglo-Saxon character. The *Analecta*, 1834, has pp. 15-18 in Anglo-Saxon character, the remainder as Old English is now commonly printed. The types used in the Psalms, 1835; *Analecta* (2d ed.), 1846; *Beowulf*, 1855; and *Anglo-Saxon Chronicle*, 1861; are entirely modern.

[2] Thos. Astle, *Origin and Progress of Writing*, London, 1784.

[3] Cott. MS. Claud. B. 4.

[4] Bodl. MS. Junius 11.

in the lower case there were twelve 'Saxon' letters.[1]   Day
subsequently cut a smaller size of 'Saxon' on a Pica body.[2]
The Dutch types surpass in clearness any Anglo-Saxon of
English casting, and are usually distinguishable by the
peculiar, horned ȝ while those of early English founding
have a flat-top ȝ. Gradually the characteristic difference disappeared, especially after the Star-Chamber decree of 1637,
which, by limiting English type-founders to four men, led
many printers to import all their types from Holland.
Almost imperceptibly Anglo-Saxon types became conventionalized, and the peculiar excellence and fame of the
Junian types, of Dutch casting, set a standard for English
founders, so that by the beginning of the eighteenth century there was no essential difference between English and
Dutch Anglo-Saxon types.[3]

   Comparatively little Old English was printed on the
Continent during the sixteenth and seventeenth centuries,[4]
and even in England the use of Anglo-Saxon types was not
without exceptions, for both Roman type and black-letter
were used for printing Old English specimens,[5] although
no full texts were so printed.

   It seems impossible to establish the actual founders of
Anglo-Saxon types between Day and Haviland, but the
following notes, principally upon individual printers known
to have used such types, may indicate their possible source.

   John Day (1540-1584) used Anglo-Saxon types in printing *A Testimonie of Antiquitie, 1566; Archaionomia*, 1568;
Actes and Monuments, 2d ed., 1570; 3d ed., 1576; 4th ed.,
1583; the Gospels, 1571; *De Antiquitate Britannicæ, 1572;*

---

[1] Anglo-Saxon letters differ from ordinary Roman type in the capitals
C, E, G, H, M, (S), W, and in lower-case d, (e), f, g, (h), (m), r, s, t, w: to
these are added ȝ þ and the abbreviations ꝥ, ꝗ. *Wen and thorn* are runic
letters, the other variants from modern type are characteristic of the period
of the manuscripts, and not of the language itself.

[2] Cf. Reed, *Old English Letter Founders*, p. 96.   [3] Cf. Plates D and E.

[4] Before Junius' *Cædmon*, Dort, 1655, there were but sporadic passages
and alphabets printed in Anglo-Saxon type on the Continent, viz.: in Camden, *Anglica*, Frankfort, 1603; Verstegan, *Restitution*, Antwerp, 1605; Parker,
De Antiq. Eccl., Hanover, 1605; Selden, *Mare Clausum*, Batavia, 1636.

[5] Vulcanius, *De Litteris et Lingua*, Bruges, 1597, and Camden, *Anglica*,
Frankfort, 1603, have the preface to Gregory's *Pastoral* in Roman type;
Camden, *Remains*, London, 1605, has two Paters in Roman type; Verstegan, *Restitution*, London, 1628 and 1634, has Old English words in black-
letter; Selden, *Janus Anglorum*, London, 1610 and 1683, has Old English
passages in black-letter.

Alfredi Regis Res Gestæ, 1574. One other book, *A Defence of Priests' Marriages*, contains specimens of this type, apparently used by another printer in Day's lifetime. The use of the types occurs in a few copies only, bearing the imprint of R. Jugge. It is reasonable to suppose, since both Day and Jugge were employed by Parker, that the archbishop had some control over the types he had procured. Jugge is not known to have done any other printing with Anglo-Saxon types, and it is more than probable that Day or his assistants set up the few sheets containing the Old English quotations. These leaves of the altered copies do not correspond in the ordinary type to similar leaves of the original issue printed by J. Kingston for Jugge.[1]

Peter Short (1598-1603) was joint assignee of Day with John Windt. He used the Day Anglo-Saxon types in the fifth edition of the *Actes and Monuments*.[2] This edition was begun by Henry Denham, and at his death Short was authorized to finish it, printing as assign of R. Day, the printer's son. An extract from the will of Ralph Newberry (partner of Denham and Binneman) throws some light on this transaction: 'And whereas I have a stocke of bookes in Stationers' Hall that belongs unto me, as the Remainder of the *Booke of Martirs*,[3] and certaine parte of and in Maister Daie and Maister Seres priviledge for printing of bokes, my will and mynde is that my said Stocke and partes in Stationers' Hall shall be sould'.[4] From this it is evident that Newberry had a share in the Day-Seres business,[5] but he apparently never used Day's Anglo-Saxon types.

William Stansby (1597-1639) bought Windt's[6] share of the Day business. He used the Day Anglo-Saxon types in printing Selden's *Eadmer*, 1623; *Titles of Honor* (second edition), 1631; and *Mare Clausum*, 1635. In the first edition of *Titles of Honor*, 1614, Stansby used a small amount

---

[1] Cf. chap. I, p. 27.

[2] The next four editions of the *Actes and Monuments*, or *Book of Martyrs*, all containing the same specimens of Old English, are printed for the Company of Stationers, evidently not with the Day types. The Anglo-Saxon type of these editions resembles Haviland's types, and substitutes a large number of Roman letters for the Anglo-Saxon characters.

[3] Foxe's *Actes and Monuments*.

[4] Cf. Plomer, *Wills of English Printers*, London, 1903.

[5] Wm. Seres, partner of Day, appointed Denham and Newberry as his executors.   [6] Windt never used Anglo-Saxon types.

of Anglo-Saxon type, unlike the Day fonts. This latter style was used in Selden's *History of Tithes*, 1618—the printer not given, but presumably Stansby.

Specimens of Anglo-Saxon types, not of the Day foundry, are met with as early as 1576, only ten years after their invention. Henry Middleton (1567-1587) used Anglo-Saxon types in printing *A Perambulation of Kent*, 1567, for Ralph Newberry. This type is Small Pica, and very poor. Evidently the printer had a very limited quantity of the type, since a Roman letter is often substituted for an Anglo-Saxon character. Edmund Bollifont printed a second edition, 1596, using the same scant type as Middleton.

Ralph Newberry (1560-1607) began using Anglo-Saxon types in printing *Eirenarcha*, 1581. He printed five editions of this book, each containing a few lines of Old English. The 1581 edition is full of typographical blunders, such as the use of Þ for ſ; ƿ for þ; δ for ð. The editions of 1591 and 1594 exhibit a much better Anglo-Saxon type, more correctly used. This improved type was used by Thomas Wright and Bonham Norton in the 1599 edition, but, curiously enough, the 1602 edition (Wright), and the succeeding editions of 1607, 1614, 1619 (for the Stationers' Company), reverted to the use of the poorer type of the 1581 edition. All these sporadic Anglo-Saxon types are Small Pica, with a flat top ð, and are not clear cut. It is evident that the English printers were, between 1576 and 1623, experimenting with these types, casting a meagre amount, and improving on it as they added to their quantity.

John Haviland (1613-1638) is the first important founder of English-style Anglo-Saxon types. He printed the *Saxon Treatise*, 1623, and the *Guide into Tongues*, 1625, with a full Anglo-Saxon character, resembling in style the experimental types of Newberry, but more carefully and clearly executed.[1] Another so-called edition of the *Saxon Treatise*, 1638, printed by E. G. for Francis Eglesfield, bookseller, is identical with the 1623 edition, and is presumably no more than a rearranging and rebinding of the original sheets, with a spurious title-page. The only E. G. who was printing at this date is Edward Griffin, Jun. The Griffins were part of an old publishing-house, dating back to 1590.[2] The Widow Griffin took Haviland into

---

[1] Cf. Plate B.

[2] Edmund Bollifont was one of the founders.

De veteri testamento.

Ðis geƿrit ƿæs to anum men geðiht ac hit mæg
ⁱþa ðeah manegum fremian.

Ælfric Abbod gret freondlice Sigƿerd æt eart
Heolon. Ic secge þe to soðan þ þe bið sƿiþe
ƿis reþe mid þeorcum sƿriceð. ꞇ se hæfð
forþgang for gode. ꞇ for populde, seðe
mid godum þeorcum hine sylfne geglengð. ꞇ þ is sƿiþe
gesƿutelod on halgum geretnissun þ þa halgan papay
þe gode þeope be eodon þ hi ƿunðfulle þænon on þissene
populde. ꞇ nu halige rindon onheofenan nicer minþþe
ꞇ heora ge mynd þurþ þunað nu ato populde for heora
anþconisse ꞇ heora. trýƿðe ƿið god. Ða gimeleasan
men þe heora lif aþpugon on ealpe iðelnisse ꞇ sƿa ge
endodon heora ge mynd is forgiten on halgum geƿri-
tum. buton þ recgað þa ealdan geretnissa heorayfelan
ðæða ꞇ þ þ þig fordemde rindon. Ðu bæde me for oft
englisepa geƿritena. ꞇ ic þe ne getiðode ealler þa
timlice ær ðam þe þu mid þeorcum þæs ge pilnodest æt
me þaða þu me bæde for godes lufon geornne þ ic þæt
ham æt þinum hore ge sƿpæce. ꞇ þuða sƿiðe mænodest
þaþa ic mid þe ƿæs þ þu miƿe geƿritabegitan ne mihtest
nu

partnership, the press being run for some years by Haviland, Robert Young, and Miles Flesher.[1]

Richard Hodgkinsonne (— 1668 ?) printed an undated edition of the *Perambulation of Kent*, using a small quantity of Anglo-Saxon type identical with Haviland's types. From an entry in the *Stationers' Registers* for July 7, 1621, we learn that Haviland and Widow Griffin had an interest in the *Perambulation of Kent*,[2] and this may relate to the Hodgkinsonne edition. The only extensive use that Hodgkinsonne ever made of Anglo-Saxon types was in the first volume of Dugdale's *Monasticon*, 1655. The only other certain use of these types by Hodgkinsonne is to be found in an Anglo-Saxon alphabet in Ben Jonson's *English Grammar*, 1640. Presumably he was the printer of the 1656 edition of the *Perambulation of Kent*.[3] In 1635 Hodgkinsonne was in trouble with the Star Chamber;[4] his presses and letters were seized, but restored. On March 21, 1637, he purchased type of Arthur Nichols, founder.[5] This Nichols was a Star-Chamber founder, and it is probable that all the types used by Haviland and Hodgkinsonne were of his founding. We are led to the supposition that there was a community of types among Haviland, Hodgkinsonne, J. Brown (*Guide into Tongues*, 1617), and J. Beale (Spelman's *Archæologus*, 1626), since their Anglo-Saxon types seem identical, as do their Italic capitals and some lower case Roman-letter peculiarities. Brown, in the printing of the first edition of the *Guide into Tongues*, used a Great Primer Anglo-Saxon alphabet of Day, beside the Haviland style Pica.[6] Since between 1637 and 1692 the Star-Chamber decree limited English type-founders to four, all Anglo-Saxon types used in the later half of the seventeenth century must have come from three sources: the Star-Chamber founders, imported type from Holland, or surviving parts of fonts cast for Day or Haviland. Between these two men, the quantity of Anglo-Saxon type

[1] All of these printers used Anglo-Saxon type.

[2] 'Joh. Haviland, Mistris Griffin entered for their Copies, by order of a Courte, holden this Daie, theis Copies following. . . . The perambulacon of Kent.' *Stat. Reg.*, 4, 55.

[3] The undated edition printed by Hodgkinsonne has identical Anglo-Saxon types with the 1656 edition, both for D. Pakeman.

[4] Plomer, *Dictionary of Printers*, pp. 93, 143.

[5] Cf. *State Papers I Chas. I*, pp. 350-53.

[6] There is but a small amount of Old English in this dictionary.

used by any printer is hardly sufficient to dignify him as a founder.

Miles Flesher (1611-1664) became a partner of Haviland and Young in the King's printing-house. They bought up the Stansby business, and presumably, with it, part of the original Day Anglo-Saxon types. James Flesher (1647?-1668?) inherited his father's business. It seems that the Fleshers printed with both Day and Haviland types. In the gloss to Wat's edition of Matthew Paris, 1640, Miles Flesher used some of the Haviland Anglo-Saxon types. The next year, 1641, Young printed the *De Sepultura*, using some Day types. James Flesher printed the *History of Tithes*, 1647, using Day types. This enables us to trace the history of the first Anglo-Saxon font for seventy-one years. In *De Quatuor Linguis*, 1650, and *Historiæ Anglicanæ X*, 1652, J. Flesher used Haviland-style type. It would seem, since they used Anglo-Saxon types sporadically, that the Flesher-Young combination had acquired enough such type to be independent of the Star-Chamber founders.[1]

Richard Badger (1602-1642) was an apprentice of P. Short, and associated in business with Richard Day. Thus he may have acquired some Day types. That which he used in printing H. Spelman's *Concilia*, 1639, and J. Spelman's *Psalterium*, 1640, is somewhat conventionalized. The Psalter required a large quantity of type, so this Badger type was probably a new font, cast by Nichols (?).

Roger Daniel (1638?—), Cambridge University printer, used a Great Primer Anglo-Saxon in Wheloc's *Bede*, 1643, and *Archaionomia*, 1644. The ᵹ of the Cambridge types differs from the horned ᵹ of the Dutch types and the flat top ᵹ of the Haviland types.[2] This was the first Anglo-Saxon type owned by a university. It is generally asserted that the Somner dictionary was not printed at Cambridge, because the University had only Great Primer types. Probably the small quantity of Pica used by John Hayes in printing Sheringham's *De Origine Gentis*, 1670, was acquired after the original font.[3] The next notable use of Anglo-Saxon types at Cambridge was a new font, 1722,

---

[1] This is assuming that the Haviland types may have been cast by Nichols before he became a Star-Chamber founder.

[2] The Paris Anglo-Saxon types used in Du Fresne's (Du Cange) *Glossarium*, 1678, closely resembles the Daniel types.

[3] Reed, *Old English Letter Founders*, asserts that Cambridge had Pica Anglo-Saxon; but there seems to be no evidence of their use before 1670.

PLATE C
Badger.

BYIERO . . . . .

Pſalmus I.

Eaꝺιꟑ   peꞃ ꞃc ꝺe ꞃe ꝼeꞃꝺe

*B*EATVS *Vir qui non abiit*
on ꟑeþeahꞇe   aꞃ�leaꞃꞃa ⁊ on
in conſilio impiorum, & *in*
ꝛeꟑe ꞃynꝼulꞃa ꞃa ꞃꞇoꝺ. ⁊
via peccatorum non ſtetit &
on þꞃymꞃeꞇle · ⸭ ꞊ ⸭ ⸭ ⸭   ꞃa   ꞃʌꞇꞽ   ac

in cathedra peſtilentiæ non ſedit. ¶ . 2 *Sed*
oꞃ   ʌ · Ꞻꞽuhꞇꞃeꞃ   ꝑιllaꞃ hꞽꞃ   ⁊   oꞃ   ʌ   hꞽꞃ
in lege Domini voluntas ejus, & *in lege ejus*
· bιꝺꞃꞧeaꝺ ꝺaꟑꞽꞃ ⁊ ꞃꞃhꞇꞺꞃ.   ⁊   bιꝺ   ꞃꝑa ꞃꝑa
meditabitur die ac nocte. ¶ 3. *Et erit tanquam*
ꞇꞃeoꝛ   ꝺʌꞇ · ꝑlaꞃꞇuꝺ   ιꞃ ꞃeh   ꞃꞽꝺe ꝑe-
lignum quod plantatum eſt ſecus decurſus a-
ꞇꞃꞃa   þ · ꝑꞃꞃꞇꞞ hꞽꞃ †ꞃꞽlꝺ oꞃ   ꞇιꝺe

· lib. Cant. cꝛꞽ
ꝺeꞃ lib. Trin.
quulmeꞃe.
· T. lauoꞃꝺe
· T. þeꞃeaþ
· T. ꟑeꞃeꞇ
· T. hleꞃ

Spelman, *Psalterium,* 1640

164

in Smith's edition (Wheloc's *Bede*). This type was Great
Primer and Pica, more conventional in style than the
Daniel types.[1] A prospectus of Wilkins' *Leges* was printed
at Cambridge in 171⅜ (same type as Smith). These are
the only two fonts of Anglo-Saxon used by Cambridge
before 1800.

There was one sporadic use of Anglo-Saxon types at
Oxford before either University possessed such types. In
1634, William Turner, Oxford University printer, issued a
second edition of Ridley's *Laws*,[2] containing two Old English quotations in Anglo-Saxon type. This type seems
identical with that used in the Hodgkinsonne undated edition of the *Perambulation of Kent*, from which the Ridley
extracts are copied. The Ridley *Laws*, 1634, bears no in-
ternal evidence of any leaves having been set up by another
printer.[3] The book thus becomes the first example of
Anglo-Saxon types used outside of London and Lambeth.[4]
Turner[5] (1624-1648) was much involved with Michael
Sparke, Sen., London bookseller (1616-1653). In 1631
Turner and Sparke were tried before the Ecclesiastical
Court Commission for printing unlicensed books, and for
the use of other men's copies. Probably Sparke borrowed
(?) the Anglo-Saxon type for Turner. There was very
little of it, for the printer was obliged occasionally to sub-
stitute Roman letters for the Anglo-Saxon ꝧ and ð, and
he uniformly substituted Roman m, a, n, e, for the Anglo-
Saxon characters.

The first authentic use of Anglo-Saxon types by Oxford
was in Somner's dictionary, 1659. As early as May 8,
1654, Junius wrote to Selden, from Amsterdam: 'In the
meane while have I here Anglo Saxonick types (I know
not whether you call them Puncheons) a cutting, and hope
they will be matriculated and cast within the space of
seven or eight weeks at the furthest. As soon as they come

[1] Wilkins, *Concilia*, Vol. I, 1737, printed by Bowyer, uses Anglo-Saxon
types of same style as Daniel's. Nichols founded for Bowyer.

[2] *Civil and Ecclesiastical Laws*, Sir Thos. Ridley, ed. by J(ohn) G(regory),
1634; cf. pp. 178-194 for specimens, which are not in 1st edition, 1607.

[3] Mr. Falconer Madan is of the opinion that the whole of Ridley
was done at Oxford. The 3d edition, Oxford (University types), 1662,
printed by W. Hall, has same extracts.

[4] Parker, *De Antiquitate Ecclesiæ Britannicæ*, Lambeth, 1572.

[5] First entry under Turner's name in the Stationers' Registers, Nov.
17, 1630; assigned for Michael Sparke, Sen., Mar. 17, 1635. Sparke dealt
mostly in law-books.

Junius.

o. Anð ic þat þ hýꞅ beboð yꞅ ece liꝼ. þa þing þe ic ꞅpꞃece. ic ꞅpꞃece Fæðeꞃ me ꞅæðe:·

C A P. X I I I.

Ðýꞃ ᵹebýꞃað on þunꞃeꞅ-ðæᵹe æꞃ Eaꞅtꞃon:·

---

1. Æꞃ þam Eaꞅteꞃ ꝼꞃeolꞅ-ðæᵹe. ꞅe Hælenð piꞅte þ hýꞅ tið com þ he polðe ꞇan oꝼ þýꞃon miðban-eaꞃðe to hiꞅ Fæðeꞃ. þa he luꝼoðe hiꞅ leoꞃning-cnihtaꞃ þæꞃon on miðban-eaꞃðe. oð enðe he hiᵹ luꝼoðe:·

2. ꞏ þa Dꞃihtneꞅ þenunᵹ þæꞃ ᵹemacuð. þa ꝼoꞃ ꞅe ðeoꝼol on Iuðaꞅ heoꞃ-Scaꞃiotheꞅ þ he hýne belæpðe:·

3. He piꞅte þ Fæðeꞃ ꞅealðe ealle þing on hiꞅ hanða. ꞏ þ he com oꝼ Loðe ymð to Loðe.

4. He aꞃaꞅ ꝼꞃam hiꞅ þenunᵹe. ꞏ leðe hiꞅ ꞃeaꝼ. ꞏ nam linen hꞃæᵹel. ꞏ beꞃðe hýne.

5. Æꝼteꞃ þam he ðyðe pæteꞃ on ꝼæt. ꞏ þꞃoh hyꞅ leoꞃninᵹ-cnihta ꝼet ꞏ ꞃiᵹðe hi mið þæꞃe lin-pæðe þe he þæꞃ mið beᵹýꞃð:·

6. Ða com he to Simone Petꞃe. anð Petꞃuꞅ cpæð to hym. Dꞃihten. alt þu þpean mine ꝼet:·

7. Se Hælenð anðꞃpaꞃoðe ꞏ cpæð to hým. þu naꞅt nu hpæt ic ðo. ac þu ꞇ ꞃýððan:·

8. Petꞃuꞅ cpæð to hym. Ne þpyhꞅt þu næꝼꞃe mine ꝼet:· Se Hælenð hym ꞅꞃpaꞃoðe ꞏ cpæð. Lýꝼ ic þe ne þpea. næꝼꞃt þu nanne ðæl mið me:·

Junius-Marshall, *Gospels*, 1665.

to my hands, I will send you some little specimen of them, to the end I might know how they will be liked in England.'[1] Nevertheless, the first Oxford types were English, founded by Nichols at a cost of £23-7s-2d.[2] They resemble the Junian types,[3] Nichols having probably obtained puncheons and matrices from Holland. With these types—Great Primer and Pica—William Hall, the University printer, set up Somner's dictionary. There is no known use of these types between their purchase in 1655 and the dictionary-printing in 1659.[4]

Among the many fonts of letters given to the University by Bishop Fell between 1666 and 1672 were the puncheons and matrices of Anglo-Saxon, both Great Primer and Pica.[5] The use of Somner and Fell types cannot be distinguished in printed books. Junius bore the expense of the types he had cut in Amsterdam for printing *Cædmon*, 1655, and the Gospels, 1665, Dort. This same letter he gave to Oxford in 1677, with the puncheons and matrices. The gift has a romantic history. The types were used in 1689, in printing Hickes' *Institutiones Grammaticæ*. After this the Junian gift seems to have been forgotten, and no further use made of it until 1698. A letter from Tanner to Charlett, August 10, 1697, relates to the episode of its re-discovery:

> Mr. Thwaites & John Hall took the courage last week to go to Dr Hyde about Junius's matrices & punchiouns, wch he gave with his books to the University. These nobody knew where they were, till Mr. Wanley discovered some of them in a hole in Dr Hydes Study. But upon Mr. Hall's asking, Dr Hyde knew nothing of them, but at last told them he thought he had some old Punchions about his study, but he did not know how they came there, and presently produces a small box full, and taking out one, he pores upon it and at last wisely tells them that these could not be what they look'd after, for they were Æthiopic: but Mr Thwaites desiring a sight of them found that which he look'd on to be

[1] Cf. Hickes, *Thesaurus*, p. xliii.

[2] Cf. Vice-chancellor's Accounts, Sept., 1655.

[3] Cf. Plate D.

[4] Cf. Rowe Mores, *English Typographical Founders*, London, 1778.

[5] Cf. *Specimen of the Several Sorts of Letter given . . . by Dr. Fell*. Oxford, 1659. The reprint of the same, 1706, mentions 'Runic and Saxon matrices of the Dutch height 135: Saxon matrices, Small Pica 16'.

Gothic, and in the box were almost all Junius's *Saxon*, *Gothic* and Runic Punchions wᶜʰ they took away wᵗʰ them and a whole oyster-barrel full of old Greek letters, which were discovered in another hole. . . .[1]

These re-discovered Anglo-Saxon types were used to print Rawlinson's edition of Alfred's *Boethius* and Thwaites' *Heptateuchus*, 1698; Hickes' *Thesaurus*, 1703-05; and Thwaites' *Grammatica*, 1711. Ingram complains of the state in which he found the Septentrional types of Junius in 1807, stating that the sets then preserved were imperfect; the common 'Saxon' character was in a tolerable state of preservation, though some of the letters were very much worn.[2]

Oxford received one other gift of Anglo-Saxon letter— namely, the Bowyer types used in Miss Elstob's *Rudiments of Grammar*, 1715. These types were especially prepared for the grammar under the following conditions. Bowyer lost all of his types in a disastrous fire, 1712 (*circa*). He had already printed a specimen of the grammar with the same type used in the Elstob *Homily*, 1709. Lord Chief Justice Parker paid for a new font of Anglo-Saxon, for which Humphrey Wanley, at Parker's request, made drawings from Old English manuscripts. Robert Andrews (Joseph Moxon's successor) attempted to cut the types according to these drawings, but was unequal to reproducing the fine pen-lines of his model. As a result, the letters were clumsy, and naturally were not used much after their initial trial. In 1753 these types were sent by William Bowyer the younger to Rowe Mores, to be presented to Oxford:

Sir,

I make bold to transmit to Oxford the Saxon Punches and Matrices which you were pleased to intimate would not be unacceptable to that learned body. It would be a great satisfaction to me if I could by these means perpetuate my obligations to that noble Personage to whose munificence I am originally indebted for them; the late Lord Chief Justice Parker, afterwards Earl of Macclesfield, who among the numerous benefactors which my father met with after his house was burnt in 1712-3 gen-

[1] Ballard MSS., Vol. 4, No. 4.

[2] Cf. Ingram, *Inaugural Lecture on the Utility of Anglo-Saxon Literature*, Oxford, 1807.

erously procured these types to be cut to enable
him to print Mrs. Elstobs Saxon Grammar. . . .
England had not then the advantage of such an
artist in letter-cutting as hath since arisen and it is
to be lamented that the execution of these is not
equal to the intention of the Noble Donor, and I
now add, to the place in which they are to be reposited, however I esteem it a peculiar happiness
that as my father received them from a great patron
of learning, his son consigns them to the greatest
seminary of it; and that he is,
> Sir,
> Your most obliged friend,
> and humble servant,
> Will. Bowyer.[1]

Rowe Mores, instead of sending the puncheons and matrices directly to Oxford, sent them instead to the Caslon
foundry to be repaired. Caslon kept them nearly five
years, when Bowyer himself transferred them to Cottrell,
who fitted them up, and cast 15 lbs. of type. In this condition Bowyer once again gave them to Rowe Mores for
transmission to Oxford. After a lapse of several years,
Bowyer discovered that the gift had not been presented,
and elicited the information from Rowe Mores that he
awaited an opportunity to transmit them. This opportunity seems not to have come until 1764, and the formal
acknowledgment was delayed until 1778—a quarter of a
century after the donation.[2] In the *Specimen* of University
type, 1794, this Anglo-Saxon appears without hint of the
real donor: 'Characteres Anglo-Saxonici per eruditam
fœminam Eliz. Elstob ad fidem codd. MSS. delineati;
quorum tam instrumentis cusoriis quam matricibus Univ.
donari curavit. E.R.M. e Collegio Regin; A.M. 1753.

> Cusoria majuscula 42 (desunt Ᵹ et þ)
> Matrices majusculæ 44
> Cusoria minuscula 37 (desunt e et ꝺ)
> Matrices minusculæ 39.'[3]

The Oxford Press, through the University's zeal in
Old English studies, has possessed more Anglo-Saxon types
than any other printing-house. At the close of the

[1] Cf. Rowe Mores, *English Typographical Founders.*

[2] Cf. Nichols, *Anecdotes of Bowyer,* 1782.

[3] A small quantity of this Elstob type is still at the Clarendon Press.

eighteenth century, it listed puncheons, 79; matrices, 83, including Small Pica, Pica, and Long Primer.[1]

Aside from the University presses, and the more important seventeenth century printers already enumerated, there were a number of printers using Anglo-Saxon types at least once. Thomas and Alice Warren and Thomas Bradayll[2] used a type which strongly resembles the Hodgkinsonne type used in Dugdale's *Monasticon*, 1655. The 1673 volume of the *Monasticon* was printed by Thomas Newcomb; the type is poor, and does not seem to be that used by the Warrens in earlier volumes. Newcomb used this same type in Dugdale's *Origines*, 1671.

Thomas Roycroft used Anglo-Saxon type once, in Sammes' *Britannia*, 1676.

William Bowyer, Senior and Junior, were the most important printers using Anglo-Saxon types in the eighteenth century, aside from the Oxford University Press. Between 1705 and 1735 they furnished seven examples of the use of Anglo-Saxon types.[3] They had two fonts, one from the Moxon-Andrews foundry,[4] destroyed in 1712, and another, cut by Robert Andrews, known as the Elstob type.

Samuel Richardson used Anglo-Saxon types once, in a brief extract[5] in Maitland's *History of St. Paul's*, 1739.

William Strahan used Anglo-Saxon types in six editions of Johnson's dictionary, 1755-1782.

The types of Edmund Allen were used in Manning's edition of Lye's dictionary, 1772.

Thomas Jones used Anglo-Saxon types in Strutt's *Chronicle*, 1778 and 1779. Also, Charles Clark used similar types in Thorkelin's edition of Rowe Mores' *Commentarius*, 1789.

Oxford, Cambridge, and London are the only places, so far as we know, where Anglo-Saxon type was used in England before 1800, and there appears to be no such type founded in Scotland before 1825. There are, of course, sporadic uses of the type in various books where the printer is not identified;[6] but they are brief and not important. Numerically, Oxford prints the most Anglo-Saxon; John Day more than any single printer, and his types have the longest traceable history. The characteristics of the Hav-

---

[1] There are 25 examples of the use of Anglo-Saxon types at Oxford, 1659-1789.

[2] Cf. Chart of Printers. [4] Cf. Plate E.

[3] Cf. Chart of Printers. [5] Charter of William.

[6] These unidentified printers do not exceed 20 in 250 years.

Bowyer

ᴀᴘᴘᴇɴᴅɪx.

ꝼan. Nıꝼ æꝼne æni-
Ꝥeꝼ manneꝼ mæð. þæt
he cunne Ꝥoð ꝼpa ꝼonð
Ꝥehepıan ꝼpa he ꝼynðe
ıꝼ. Ac hıt ıꝼ þeah une
ealꝟa þeanꝼ þ̵ ꝟe Ꝥe-
oꝟnlıce hım þeopıan.
ꝣ ðenıan, þæꝼ ðe ꝟe
maꝤon ꝣ cunnon.

night. It is not in the
power of any Man, to
know how to praiſe God
equally to his worth.
Yet is it the duty of
every one of us dili-
gently to Serve and
worſhip him, with our
beſt Abilities and Un-
derſtanding.

DE * ꝂATUTINALE
OFFIꝆIO.
ON DꝶELRED
ꝂAN SLEAL LOD
hepıan.

† *Of the Morning Ser-
vice.*

At Day-break Men
ought to praiſe God, as
David

pleat; in the Gothic ᚾᚺᛏᚢᛉ ſignifies the Morning,
and ᛅ᛬ᚲᛇ᛬ᚭ in the Runic Lexicon is *vigilia matutina,* the
Morning Watch, which will agree with the foregoing conjecture, for as ſoon as the four and twenty Hours are out, and
the Civil Day is finiſh'd, the Morning begins; for Example,
we ſay nine, ten, eleven, and twelve a Clock at Night, but
then begin again with one, two, three in the Morning. Un-
leſs it ſhall ſeem more reaſonable to derive ᚾᚺᛏᚢᛉ,
and ᛅ᛬ᚲᛇ᛬ᚭ or Uhꝿan, from ᛉᛏᛅᚾ *metuere,*
timere, to fear, which makes ᛁᛒᚺᛏᛖᛉᚾᚾ. *timo-*

Elstob, *Saxon Devotions,* 1709.

iland types among English fonts, and the Junian Dutch types, seem to determine the style of all Anglo-Saxon letters. Early in the nineteenth century, the question arose of rationalizing the printing of Old English,[1] and the fancy of the editor determined the matter. We find examples of the use of the Anglo-Saxon character as late as 1875.[2] One utilitarian reason which may be assigned for the decline of the practice lies in a peculiarity of the prevailing Anglo-Saxon types. They were mostly of Dutch height, and could not be fitted into line with the prevailing height of early nineteenth-century types.

Before the Star-Chamber decree of 1637, it was the habit of each printer to do his own founding. The restriction placed on founding was removed in 1692, but the custom of special founders was fairly established, so that we must take into account the founders who may have furnished the printers with Anglo-Saxon types.[3]

Beginning with the original Star-Chamber founders, Arthur Nichols[4] is the only one who cast Anglo-Saxon types. Joseph Moxon (1659-1683), whose letter forms part of the Robert Andrews[5] foundry, was his successor. John Grover and his son Thomas, *circa* 1700, cut Anglo-Saxon Great Primer and Pica.[6] The foundry passed to Grover's daughter, who refused to sell it to John James, and for thirty years it was shut up, and used only by Richard Nutt, Grover's son-in-law, who cast for himself. It is uncertain whether or not he cast any Anglo-Saxon letters. This foundry passed to John James in 1758. Robert Andrews included the Moxon foundry, and cut Anglo-Saxon Pica in 1706. His foundry passed to Thomas James in 1733. James was an apprentice to Robert Andrews; he began business for himself in 1710. His son John succeeded him in 1736. His foundry consisted of the united letters of the Glovers, Moxon, Andrews, Head, Mitchell, Iloe, and miscellaneous letters of forgotten origin. James made the following catalogue of his learned-language letter in 1767:

[1] Cf. Ingram, *Inaugural Lecture.*

[2] *Anglo-Saxon Paschal Homily*, printed by John Russell Smith, London. 1875.

[3] Such information is obtainable only from the specimens of the principal foundries.

[4] Probably the founder for Haviland, Hodgkinsonne, and Cambridge-Wheloc types.

[5] Andrews founded for Bowyer.

[6] In 1700 the Grovers had Great Primer Anglo-Saxon and Pica, 30.

Anglo-Saxon—Double Pica, Great Primer, English Small Pica, Long Primer, Brevier.[1] James was the last of the old block-founders.

Of the movable founders, William Caslon, junior (1720-1763?) founded Anglo-Saxon Pica, Long Primer, and Brevier. His *Specimen*, 1766, includes of Anglo-Saxon: English, Caslon II; Pica, Caslon I; Long Primer, Caslon I; Brevier, Caslon II. Caslon III, *Specimen*, 1803, exhibits English, Pica, Brevier. Caslon IV, *Specimen*, 1825, exhibits English, Pica, Long Primer, and Brevier.[2]

Nym, *Specimen*, 1824, exhibits Double Pica, Great Primer, English, Pica, Small Pica, Long Primer, Brevier.

Figgins, *Specimen*, 1825, exhibits Pica, Small Pica, Long Primer, Brevier.

Andrew and Alexander Wilson, Glasgow, *Specimen*, 1825, exhibit English, Pica, Small Pica, Long Primer, Brevier.

There are two examples of the Anglo-Norman character of the *Doomsday Book* in the eighteenth century; one by Cotteral and the other by Joseph Jackson, 1783.[3]

(b)
CHART OF PRINTERS USING ANGLO-SAXON TYPES, 1566-1800

The following chart indicates the use made of Anglo-Saxon types in England between 1566 and 1800. Those marked * are full texts printed in the character; ° indicates extracts varying in length, but exhibiting a considerable amount of Anglo-Saxon type. The remainder exhibit sporadic uses of the character:

Date of Publication	Title	Author or Editor	Printer
1566	* A Testimonie of Antiquitie	Parker	J. Day
1567	A Defence of Priests' Marriages	Parker	A Jugge (Day types ?)
1568	* Archaionomia	Lambarde	J. Day

[1] Rowe Mores found the Anglo-Saxon Double Pica, Pica, Long Primer, &c., to be missing in 1778. Reed asserts that the Great Primer was cut by Grover, and the Long Primer by Andrews.

[2] Brevier does not seem to have been used except in specimens.

[3] The Jackson types used in a facsimile printed by Nichols, 1783, deposited in the British Museum.

Oxford.

84 ÆLFREDI REGIS

onluᴛan. Ða ıc þa ðıſ eall ᵹemunðe. þa punðnoðe ıc
[1] ſpıðe þana [2] ᵹoðena [3] pıᴛena þe [4] ᵹıu pænon [5] ᵹeonð
Anᵹel cẏnn. ꝛ þa bec be ꝼullan ealla [6] ᵹeleopnoð hæꝼ-
ðon. þæᴛ [7] hı hıopa þa [8] nanne ðæl nolðon on hıopa
[9] æᵹen ᵹeðıoðe penðan. Ac ıc þa ſona eꝼᴛ me [10] ſel-
ſum anðpẏnðe ꝛ cpæð. hıe ne pænðon þæᴛ [11] ᴛe æſne
[12] men [13] ſceolðon ſpa þecceleaſe [14] peopðan ꝛ ſıo lan
ſpa oðꝼeallan. ſon ðæne pılnunᵹa hıe hıᴛ ſonleᴛon
ꝛ polðon ðæᴛ hen [15] þẏ mana pıſðom on [16] lonðe pæne
ðẏ pe ma [17] ᵹeðıoða cuðon. Ða ᵹemunðe ıc hu ſıo æ
pæſ æneſᴛ on Ebneıſc ᵹeðıoðe ſunðen. ꝛ [18] eꝼᴛ þa
[19] þa [20] hıe Cnecaſ [21] ᵹeleopnoðon. þa penðon [22] hı [23] hıe
on hıopa [24] æᵹen ᵹeðıoðe ealle. ꝛ eac ealle [25] oðne bec.
Anð eꝼᴛ Læðen pane [26] ſpa ſame. ſıðð an [27] hı hıe [28] ᵹeleopnoðon. [29] hı hıe penðon ealle ðunh ſıne pealh ſᴛo-
ðaſ on hıopa aᵹen [30] ᵹeðeoðe. [31] ꝛ eac [32] ealla oðna Cnı-
ſᴛena ðıoða ſumne ðæl hıopa on hıopa aᵹen ᵹeðıoðe
penðon. ſon ðẏ me [33] ðẏncð beᴛne. ᵹıſ ıop [34] ſpa ðẏncð.
þæᴛ pe eac [35] ſum bec. ða [36] þe [37] nıð beðẏnſeſᴛa
[38] ſıen eallum monnum ᴛo [39] pıᴛahne. þæᴛ pe þa on

---

1 ſpıðe ſpıðe *Jun.* 2 ᵹoðna *Alt.* ᵹoðena *Edd. P. & C.*
3 pıoᴛona *Hatt.* 4 ᵹeo *Edd. P. & C.* 5 ᵹıonð *Hatt*
6 ᵹeliopnoð *Hatt.* 7 *Deeſt Edd. P & C.* 8 nænne *H*
9 aᵹen *Hatt. & Alt.* 10 ſẏlſum *Alt. Edd. P.*
11 *Deeſt Edd. P. & C.*

Wise, Asser's *Annales Ælfredi Regis*, 1772.

Appendix III   175

Date of Publication	Title	Author or Editor	Printer
1570	° Actes and Monuments...Foxe.........J. Day		
	1576..............................J. Day		
	1583..............................J. Day		
	1596..............................J. Day		
	1610..............................P. Short for assigns of R. Day (Day types ?)		
	1631..............................For Sta. Co.		
	1641..............................For Sta. Co.		
	1684..............................For Sta. Co.		
1571	* Gospels................Foxe.........J. Day		
1572	° De Antiquitate Britan- nicæ Ecclesiæ........Parker.......(J. Day ?)		
	1605..............................Typis Wechelianis [Hanover]		
	1729................re-ed. by S. Drake...W. Bowyer		
1574	* Alfredi Regis Res Gestæ..............Parker.......J. Day		
1576	° Perambulation of Kent...Lambarde....H. Middleton for R. Newberry		
	1596..............................E. Bollifont		
	n. d..............................R. Hodgkinsonne for D. Pakeman (Haviland types ?)		
	1656..............................For D. Pakeman and M. Walbancke (Hodgkinsonne-Haviland types ?)		
1581	Eirenarcha.............Lambarde....H. Bynneman and R. Newberry		
	1582..............................Newberry		
	1588..............................Newberry		
	1591..............................Newberry		
	1594..............................Newberry		
	1599..............................Tho Wright and B. Norton (Newberry types ?)		
	1602..............................Tho Wright		
	1607..............................For Sta. Co.		
	1610..............................For Sta. Co.		
	1614..............................For Sta. Co.		

Date of Publication	Title	Author or Editor	Printer
1603	° Anglica, Normannica	Camden	impensis Claudij Marnij & hæredum johannis Aubij. [Frankfort]
1605	Restitution of Decayed Intelligence	Verstegan	Robert Bruney [Antwerp]
1610	Janus Anglorum	Selden	T. S. for J. Helme
	1683		For Tho. Basset and R. Chiswell
1614	° Titles of Honour	Selden	W. Stansby
	1631		W. Stansby for R. Whittakers (Day types ?)
1617	Guide into Tongues	Minsheu	J. Brown
	1625		J. Haviland
1618	° History of Tithes	Selden	(W. Stansby ?)
1623	* Saxon Treatise	L'Isle	J. Haviland for H. Selie
	1638		E. G. (Edw. Griffin ?) for Francis Eglesfield
1623	Eadmeri Monachi Historiæ,	Selden	W. Stansby (Day types ?)
1626	Archæologus, part 1	H. Spelman	J. Beale
	1664	Completed by Dugdale	Alice Warren
	1687		Thos. Bradayll (Warren types ?)
1634	Civil and Ecclesiastical Laws (Ridley)	Gregory	Wm. Turner [Oxford] (Hodgkinsonne-Haviland types ?)
	1662		W. Hall for E. Forest [Oxford] (University types, Somner ?)
1635	° Mare Clausum	Selden	W. Stansby for R. Meighen (Day types ?)
	1636		Lugdivi Bativornii
	1638		W. Stansby for R. Meighen (Day types ?)

Date of Publication	Title	Author or Editor	Printer
	1652................English trans. by M. Nedham		
	1663................ " "		For A. Kemble and E. Thomas
1639	Concilia, Decreta, part 1	H. Spelman...R. Badger	
1640	English Grammar.......Ben Jonson...R. Hodgkinsonne (Haviland types ?)		
1640	Matthew Paris.........Wats........M. Flesher		
	1684.............................		(?)
1640	* Psalterium.............J. Spelman...R. Badger		
1641	De Sepultura..........H. Spelman...R. Young (Day types ?)		
1643	* Historiæ Ecclesiasticæ Gentis Anglorum......Wheloc.......Roger Daniel (Cambr. types)		
1644	* Archaionomia..........Wheloc......Roger Daniel (Cambr. types)		
1647	History of Tithes.......H. Spelman...For P. Stephens		
1650	De Quatuor Linguis.....Casaubon.....J. Flesher		
1652	Historiæ Anglicanæ Scriptores X.........Twysden.....J. Flesher		
1655	* Cædmonis Monachi Paraphrasis Poetica......Junius		Christopher Cunrad [Amsterdam] (Junius types)
1655	Monasticon, vol. 1......Dugdale......R. Hodgkinsonne		
	1661, vol. 2......................Alice Warren		
	1673, vol. 3......................T. Newcomb and Abel Roper		
	1682, vol. 1, reprint...............		(?)
	1722-23.............Re-ed. by Stephens...		(?)
1658	History of St. Paul's......Dugdale......Tho. Warren		
	1716.............................Geo. James for J. Bowyer		
1659	Dictionarium Saxonico-Latino-Anglicum......Somner......W. Hall [Oxford] (Univ. types)		
1660	Gavelkind..............Somner....For R. & W. Leybourne		
	1726................Re-ed. by Kennett....(Bowyer types ?)		

Date of Publication	Title	Author or Editor	Printer
1663	Gavelkind..............Taylor.......		For J. Starkey (Hodgkinsonne-Haviland types?)
1665	* Quatuor D. N. Jesu Christi Euangeliorum	Marshall and Junius.......	Excudebant Henricus et Johannis Essæ [Dort] (Junius types)
	1684.............................		Excudebant Henricus et Johannes Essæ [Amsterdam] (Junius types)
1666	Origines Juridicales......Dugdale......		F. & T. Warren
	1671.............................		Tho. Newcomb
	1681.............................		(?)
1670	De Anglorum Gentis Origine.............Sheringham...		John Hayes [Cambridge]
1676	° Britannia Antiquia Illustrata............Sammes......		Tho. Roycroft
1678	° Ælfredi Magni Vita.....J. Spelman, ed. by C. Ware and O. Walker........		[Oxford] (Univ. types)
	1709.................Re-ed. by Hearne.....		[Oxford] (Univ. types)
1678	Glossarium ad Scriptores	Du Fresne....	[Paris]
	1733.............................		[Paris] (Same types)
1684	Discourses of Law Terms	H. Spelman...	For Matt. Gillyflower (Oxford types ?)
1689	A Seasonable Treatise....	(?)	For J. Robinson
1689	° Institutiones Grammaticæ Anglo-Saxonicæ	Hickes.......	[Oxford] (Junius types)
1689	Gazophylacium	(?)	E. H. and W. H.
1690	Thesaurus Linguæ Anglo-Saxonicæ Dictionario Gul. Someri..	Benson.......	[Oxford] (Univ. types)

Date of Publication	Title	Author or Editor	Printer
1690	Historia Dogmatica.....	Ussher, ed. by H. Wharton	Types R. R. impensis R. Chiswell
1691	Anglica Sacra, vol. 1.....	H. Wharton...	Impensis R. Chiswell
1691	° Historia Britannica......	Tho. Gale....	[Oxford] (Univ. types)
1692	* Chronicon Saxonicum....	Gibson.......	[Oxford] (Univ. types)
1693	History of Roman Ports and Forts............	Somner, ed. by Brome.....	[Oxford] (Univ. types)
1698	* Heptateuchus..........	Thwaites.....	[Oxford] (Junius types)
1698	* An. Manl. Sever. Bœthi Consolationis Philosophiæ...............	C. Rawlinson	[Oxford] (Junius types)
1698	Reliquiæ Spelmannianæ	Gibson.......	[Oxford] (Univ. types)
1699	° Hormesta Pauli Orosii...	W. Elstob....	[Oxford, printed, not published] (Univ. types)
1700?	* Specimen pages of Gregory's Pastoral Care....	Thwaites.....	[Oxford ?]
1700	Oratio Dominica........	(?)	D. Brown and W. Keblewhite
1701	° Sermo Lupi Episcopi.....	W. Elstob....	[Oxford]
1701	° Vocabularium Anglo-Saxonicum..........	Benson.......	[Oxford]
1703-05	° Thesaurus.............	Hickes.......	[Oxford] (Junius types ?)
1705	° Several letters between Dr. Hickes and a Popish Priest...........	Hickes, W. Elstob..	W. Bowyer
	1715............................		(?)
	1727............................		(?)
1708	Conspectus (of Hickes' Thesaurus)..........	Wotton......	W. Bowyer
1708	Notæ in A. S. Nummos...	Thwaites.....	[Oxford]
1709	* An English-Saxon Homily.......	E. Elstob.....	W. Bowyer

Date of Publication	Title	Author or Editor	Printer
1711	° Grammatica, Anglo-Saxonica............Thwaites.....[Oxford]		
1713	Oratio Dominica....... (?)		A. D. Brown
1713	Oratio Dominica........Chamberlayne		W. & D. Goerli [Amsterdam]
1715	* English-Saxon Homilies of Ælfric............E. Elstob.....[Oxford, printed, not published]		
1715	Rudiments of Grammar..E. Elstob.....Bowyer For the English-Saxon Tongue		
171⅜	° Proposals for printing Wilkins' Leges Anglo-Saxonicæ........................[Cambridge] (Univ. types)		
1720	* Textus Roffensis	Hearne.......[Oxford]	
1721	* Leges Anglo-Saxonicæ...	Wilkins......W. Bowyer	
1722	* Historiæ Ecclesiasticæ...	Smith.......[Cambridge] (New University types)	
1722	° Annales Rerum Gesta-rum Ælfredi Magni....Wise.........[Oxford]		
1723	° Hemengi Chartularium...Hearne.......[Oxford]		
1726	History and Antiquities of Canterbury.......J. Dart.......J. Cole		
1726	Introduction to English Grammar...........Henley.......J. Roberts		
1726	Seldeni Opera..........Wilkins......W. Bowyer		
1735	Wotton's Conspectus of Hickes' Thesaurus....Trans. by		
		Shelton....For the author (Bowyer types)	
	1737............................		W. Bowyer
1737	° Concilia Magnæ Britan-niæ, vol. 1..........Wilkins......W. Bowyer		
1739	History of London......Maitland.....S. Richardson		
1739	Inquiry into the Founda-tion of Westminster...Widmore.....For J. Story		
1743	° Etymologicum Anglica-num (Junius).........Lye..........[Oxford]		
1751	History of St. Peter's Westminster..........Widmore.....J. Fox		
1754	* Figuræ et Cædmonis Monachi Paraphrseos Notæ...............Rowe Mores [Oxford ?]		

Date of Publication	Title	Author or Editor	Printer
1755	English Dictionary	Johnson	W. Strahan
	1755-56		W. Strahan
	1765		W. Strahan
	1773		W. Strahan
	1784		(?)
	1785		(?)
1767	Proposals for printing a Dictionary, Anglo-Saxon and English	(Manning ?)	(?)
1772	° Dictionarium Saxonico et Gothico-Latinum, auctori Eduardo Lye	Manning	Typis E. Allen
1773	* Orosius	Barrington	Bowyer and Nichols
1778	° Chronicle of England	Strutt	Tho. Jones
	1779		Tho. Jones
1788	King Alfred's Will	Manning	[Oxford]
1789	° Edwardi Rowei Moresi, Commentarius de Æl-frico	Thorkelin	Charles Clark

APPENDIX IV

LEARNED SOCIETIES AND LIBRARIES IN LONDON, CONTRIBUTING TO OLD ENGLISH SCHOLARSHIP BEFORE 1800

It is to be lamented in turnynge ouer of the superstycyouse monasteryes, so lytle respecte was had to theyr lybraryes. . . . A greate nombre of them whych purchased those superstycyouse mansyons, reserued of those lybrarye bokes, . . . some to scoure theyr candelstyckes, and some to rubbe their bootes. Some they solde to the grossers and sope sellers, & some they sent ouer see to the bokebynders, not in small nombre, but at tymes whole shyppes full, to the wonderynge of the foren nacyons. . . . Oure posteryte maye wele curse thys wycked facte of our age, thys unreasonable spoyle of Englandes most noble Antiquytees, vnlesse they be stayed in tyme, and by the art of pryntynge be brought into a nombre of coppyes. . . . Steppe you fourth now last of all, ye noble men and women (as there are in these dayes a great nombre of you most nobyllye lerned, prayse be to God for it) and showe your naturall noble hartes to your nacyon. . . . As ye fynde a notable Antyquyte, suche as are the hystoryes of Gildas and Nennius amonge the Brytaynes, Stephanides and Asserius among the Englyshe Saxons, lete them anon be imprinted, and so brynge them into a nombre of coppeyes, both to their and your owne perpetuall fame.[1]

The same motives that actuated Bale in the preparation of his catalogue,[2] and which he so eloquently set forth in his preface to Leland's *Laboryouse Journey*, stirred a group of scholarly men, headed by Archbishop Parker, to organize themselves into an informal society. Pre-

---

[1] Bale, Preface to Leland's *Laboryouse Journey, 1549.*

[2] *Illustrium Maioris Britanniæ Scriptorum Summarium*, Ipswich, 1548, and Wessel, 1549. Enlarged edition, Basle, 1557-59. Cf. Lane Poole's edition, Oxford, 1902.

sumably this organization began in 1572. In 1589 the members applied to the Queen for a charter of incorporation, and for the use of a public building to house their library.[1] A rough draft of the petition discloses the nature of the society to have been 'An Academy for the study of Antiquity and History', under a President, two Librarians, and a number of Fellows, with a body of statutes, the library to be called the Library of Queen Elizabeth, and to be well furnished with scarce books, original charters, muniments, and other manuscripts; the members to take the oath of supremacy, and another to serve the library.[2] Several reasons were urged for the incorporation of such a society: 'That there are many monuments worthy of observation, whereof the originals are extant in the hands of some private gentleman; and also divers other excellent MSS, whereof there is no record: which by this means shall have public and safe custody, for use when occassion shall serve. . . . This Society will not interfere with the Universities, as tending to the preservation of History and Antiquities, whereof the Universities, long buried in Arts, take no regard. The more civilized nations, as Germany, Italy and France, take great care to encourage this kind of learning, by public lectures, libraries and academies.' Other clauses of the petition recite the Society's intention to preserve copies of the charters of various kings, and the intention to study modern languages as a means of fitting men for public offices.

The Society was not incorporated, perhaps owing to the Queen's death, but existed as a private organization until James I dissolved it, having refused a charter. About 1617 proposals were made to the Marquis of Buckingham for its revival, the Society to meet at Westminster and Windsor, to have one general chapter in a year, and four quarterly dinners. Nothing definite seems to have come of this plan, and the Society was in abeyance until the eighteenth century. Among the members of this earlier period were such men as Camden, Carew, Cotton, Lambarde, Stow, Spelman, and Thynne. For a time the turmoil of the civil wars threatened to complete the destruction of national monuments begun at the Dissolution, yet

---

[1] Their meeting-place for twenty years was the house of Sir Robert Cotton.

[2] MS. Cott. Faustina E. V., ff. 67, 68, and *Archæologia*, Vol. 1. The petition was signed by Sir Robert Cotton, Sir John Doddridge, and Sir James Lee.

such men as Selden, Dugdale, Spelman, D'Ewes, Ussher, Laud, Wheloc, and Somner went on collecting, transcribing, and publishing from the stores of national records that had survived. To what extent these men were bound by ties similar to those of the original Society of Antiquaries, is difficult to say. The definite revival of the Society dates from 1707. Some memoranda in the writing of Humphrey Wanley contain the following:[1]

> *Friday,* 5 *December, 1707.* Mr Talman, Mr Bagford and Mr Wanley mett together, and agreed to meet together each Friday, in the evening, by six of the Clock, upon pain of forfeiture of six pence. Agreed that we will meet each Friday night at the Bear Tavern in the Strand, till we shall order otherwise.
>
> *Friday,* 12 *December,* 1707. Agreed that the business of this Society shall be limited to the object of Antiquities, and more particularly to such things as may illustrate, or relate to the History of Great Britain. Agreed that by the subject of Antiquities and History of Great Britain, we understand such things only as shall precede the reign of James the First, King of England. Provided that upon any new discovery of antient coins, Sepulchres, or other remains of antient workmanship, which may be communicated to us, we reserve to ourselves the liberty of conferring upon them. Agreed that the business of this Society shall be adjourned, or broken off, at Ten of the Clock at the furthest. Agreed that while we shall meet at a Tavern,[2] no person shall be obliged to pay for more than he shall call for.
>
> *January* 9. Agreed that Mr Le Neve be desired to be Chairman till our number shall exceed ten.
>
> *January* 23. Twas proposed that any Member in this Society might be free to make known any doubts that may arise in his reading of old books, charters, etc, in order to receive satisfaction, if any other member should have meet with further light

---

[1] Harl. MS. 7055.

[2] Between Jan. 2, 1708, and Feb. 20, when the Wanley memoranda close, the meetings were held at the Young Divel Tavern, Fleet Street, and the following names proposed for membership: Le Neve, Holmes (Tower Record-Keeper), Madox, Batteley, Elstob, Stebbing, Hare, Sanderson (Clerk of Rolls), and Bowchier.

in such case. This was agreed to. Twas further propos'd that if any member should happen to make any observation in his reading, or research of Antiquities, which he should think might be of use, he might be free to communicate the same. This was agreed to.

This little band seems to have existed somehow for about ten years, during which time Wanley laid the Society's plans before the Earl of Oxford, whose house was thought a proper meeting-place, because of his library. Their idea was to search out and preserve monumental inscriptions, painting, engraving, music, with an attempt to restore ancient methods, to explain obscurities in all antiquities; correspond with learned antiquaries abroad; travel to inspect books, manuscripts, fortifications, castles, churches, houses, tombs, inscriptions, epitaphs, and glass, and to buy curiosities for the Society. The dues of the Society were to help defray the expense of printing and engraving such things as they saw fit, one copy to be given each member, and the rest to be sold for their benefit. The founders January 171⅞ were: Peter Le Neve, Pres.; William Stukeley, Sec.; Samuel Gale, Treas.; John Talman, Director; Edward Alexander, Roger Gale, John Hare, George Holmes, James Mickleton, William Becket, John Chicheley,—Wrottesley,—Pavey, Humphrey Wanley, Robert Sanderson, William Nicholas, Maurice Johnson, Samuel Knight, George Vertue, Brown Willis, Robert Stephens, John Harwood.[1]

Among the Wanley memoranda are entries of the intention to print the *Doomsday Book*, the *Red Book of the Exchequer*, a *History of the Great Abbies and their Dissolution*, and the *Parliament Rolls*. The want of such books as these is noted:[2] '*History of the Jews in England;* a *Glossary*, including Somner, Spelman, Crowel and new words from Charters and other manuscripts; a complete *Anglo-Saxon Bible;* a *Dictionary* fixing the English language as the French and Italian; a body of *Saxon Laws* and *Homilies;* a *Cento-Saxonicus* and a *Britannia-Saxonica*, desired by Dr. Hickes.'

One other organization that materially helped Old English scholarship was the Record Commission. Originally the Tower of London held the Chancery Records, which were fairly well kept, but the Exchequer Records

---

[1] Cf. *Archæologia*, London, 1770, pp. xxv ff.

[2] Cf. above, and Harleian MS. 7055.

were much scattered. In the seventeenth century the State Paper Office was established, but not until Thomas Rymer published his *Fœdera*, in the reign of Queen Anne, did the public really become aware of the condition of its national records. The great Cottonian fire in 1731 roused them to action. A Parliamentary report in 1800, concerning public records in England and Scotland, resulted in the establishment of the Record Commission, renewed each year until 1837, when the Public Record Office succeeded it. Although the Record Commission was often mismanaged, it did much for the arrangement, preservation, and publication of national antiquities, such as the Doomsday Book and the Parliament Rolls.[1]

Libraries in London before the establishment of the British Museum were not easily accessible to the public, nor were the books properly cared for or catalogued.

The Royal Library had received many books as presents from abroad, after the invention of printing; it was especially the custom to make such a New Year's gift.[2] This library had a vagrant existence.[3] In the reign of Henry VIII, part of it was removed to Greenwich, part taken to the Treasury, other portions stored at Whitehall, Hampton Court, and Windsor. In the reign of Edward VI additions were made by Cheke and Ascham, and a chapel adjoining the Guildhall was used for storing manuscripts,[4] consisting of records, charters, laws, privileges, acts of common council, etc. Neither Mary nor Elizabeth did much to increase the Royal Library.[5] In 1759, George II transferred the collection, then gathered in St. James' Palace, to the British Museum. The collection contained the libraries of Lord Lumley, Arundel, Cranmer, Casaubon, and the collections of Leland.

---

[1] Among societies for similar publication of early English literature and history in the first decades of the nineteenth century may be mentioned Roxburghe Club, 1812; Royal Society of Literature, 1825; Philological Society, Cambridge, 1830; Surtees Society, 1834; Camden Society, 1838.

[2] Leland intended his *Laboryouse Journey* for such a gift.

[3] Cf. Edwards, *Memoirs of Libraries*, London, 1901, and *Gentleman's Magazine*, April, May, 1834.

[4] Stow accuses the Duke of Somerset of 'borrowing' five cartloads of these books to furnish his house in the Strand!

[5] Elizabeth combined the office of library-keeper with that of 'Distiller of Odoriferous Herbs'; he got more salary as perfumer than he did as librarian.

At Lambeth Palace the oldest books belonged to the Earl of Leicester, and the library was greatly augmented by the archbishops, but lost valuable collections by the gifts of Parker to Cambridge, and of Laud, Ussher, and Sheldon to Oxford.

Sion College, primarily a theological library, was long distinguished as the only public library within the walls of the city of London. It was very popular, because of its convenient yet secluded location. Many of its books were destroyed in the great fire of 1666.

Gresham College acquired a considerable library from the fellows of the Royal Society, mostly books from the Earl of Arundel's collection, gathered while ambassador to Vienna.

Westminster Abbey had a library, furnished chiefly by Dr. Williams the Dean, who opened it for public use during the collegiate year, from 9 to 12 and from 2 to 4. Part of this collection was destroyed in the Cottonian fire.

Dr. Tenison, Archbishop of Canterbury, built a library near St. Martin's-in-the-Fields in 1683, and furnished it with modern books for the use of students, any of whom might have free access by registering their names and addresses.

The libraries of Lincoln's Inn, Gray's Inn, and the Middle Temple, consisted mostly of law-books and some special collections relating to English history.

The collegiate libraries of Oxford and Cambridge, together with the British Museum, have gradually absorbed the great private collections, and many of the treasures from cathedral libraries. The three great sources of Old English manuscripts were Archbishop Parker's collection, which is deposited in Cambridge, Archbishop Laud's in Oxford, and the Cotton collection in the British Museum.

The Cotton Library was the most notable private collection in England. Its founder, Sir Robert Cotton, began collecting in 1588. 'He was born', says Edwards, 'too late to share at first hand in the spoil of the old monastic libraries, yet early enough to profit by the many precious opportunities which the necessity or the avarice, the misfortunes or the death of early antiquaries, opened up in rich abundance.'[1] He was particularly interested in collecting Old English manuscripts, and gave his fellow antiquaries free use of his books. D'Ewes, in his *Autobiography*, says of him:[2]

[1] Edwards, *Memoirs of Libraries*.

[2] D'Ewes, *Autobiography*, pp. 38 ff.

I have borrowed many precious manuscripts of him, being chiefly led, out of a virtuous emulation of him at first, to the study of records, and to the treasuring and storing up of ancient coins, and elder or later manuscripts and autographs, as well as original letters of state, as old deeds and writings. I enjoyed many hours of discourse with him, and found him to be admirably skilled in the polity and government of the State and Church England; nay, so full he was almost of all variety of knowledge in that kind, as his tongue being unable to utter his inward conceits and notions fast enough, it would often enforce him to long stuttering when he endeavoured to speak exceeding fast. . . . There was one Richard James, a short, red-headed, high coloured fellow, a master of Arts, who had some time resided in Oxford, and had afterwards travelled —an atheistical, profane scholar, but otherwise witty and moderately learned. He had so screwed himself into the good opinion of Sir Robert Cotton, as whereas at first he had only permitted him the use of some of his books, at last, some two or three years before his decease, he bestowed the custody of his whole library on him, and he being a needy, sharking companion and very expensive, like old Ralph Starkie, when he lived, let out or lent out Sir Robert Cotton's most precious manuscripts for money to any that would be his customers, which Sir Robert was wont to lend freely to his noble and loving friends.

His policy was somewhat restricted by his son and grandson, partly because the political changes of the civil wars made it expedient not to advertise the possession of some books in their possession,[1] and also because many valuable books were never returned when borrowed.[2] D'Ewes complained that Sir Thomas having promised to 'lend me some manuscripts I should need for the furthering of the public work I was about; yet even when I sent to

[1] Sir Robert Cotton was haled before the Star Chamber in 1629 for the publication of a state document, lent unknown to him. For a time his library was locked, and a guard set upon his house.

[2] 'The same liberty which my father gave to the learned Mr. Selden, I give to you. But Mr. Selden was too free lending out books, which after his death were never returned.' John Cotton to Dr. Thos. Smith, April, 1693.

him but for one old book of *Saxon Charters*, into which were fastened and pasted divers originals or autographs, which he had particularly promised to communicate to me, he put me off with so many frivolous excuses or feigned subterfuges, as I forebore further troubling any messengers.'[1] Dr. Thomas Smith guarded the Cottonian collections even more jealously, and the admission of scholars at the end of the seventeenth century depended largely upon his caprice.[2] Finally, in accordance with the desire of Sir John Cotton, an Act of Parliament in 1700 provided that this library should be preserved under the name of Cotton, and governed by a board of trustees. In 1707 Sir Hans Sloane wrote to Dr. Charlett of a project to unite the Royal, the Cotton, and the Royal Society libraries. This scheme was practically realized fifty years later, when the Sloane bequest added the Arundel manuscripts from the Royal Society to the Cottonian and Royal libraries in the British Museum. In 1712 the Cotton library was moved to Essex House in the Strand, and again in 1730 to Ashburnham House. On Saturday, October 23, 1731, a fire broke out, which greatly damaged or wholly destroyed parts of this famous collection.[3] The nation had been quite oblivious of the condition and housing of its treasures up to the time of this fire. Steps were then taken to better conditions, and the Cottonian collection finally passed to the newly established British Museum.

Robert Harley, Earl of Oxford, began collecting with a considerable purchase of books in 1705. Like Cotton, he was particularly interested in manuscripts illustrative of English history. In ten years he accumulated 2500 manuscripts, including some that had belonged to Foxe, Stow, and D'Ewes.[4] Edward Harley, the second earl, increased both the manuscript and the printed collections to about 400,000 separate titles. Of these, when offered for sale by the heirs, the nation acquired the manuscript portions for £10,000. The Cottonian and Harleian collections in the

---

[1] D'Ewes, *Autobiography*, 43.

[2] Cf. Appendix I, Nos. 7, 9, 10, 12, 14.

[3] At the outbreak of the fire, the manuscripts numbered 958. Of these, 114 were reported to be lost, burnt, or seriously damaged, and 98 others less seriously damaged.

[4] D'Ewes had transcribed many records that he could not purchase, and his will requested that his books should never be shut away from lovers of learning.

British Museum represent the greatest collection of material
relating to Old English.

The English nation has been often reproached by antiquaries for its careless treatment of vast stores of rare
books, and the complaint seems just when we consider the
state of things at the end of the seventeenth century.
Nicolson, in his *Historical Library*, 1696, writing of the
Lambeth, Cotton, Oxford, and Cambridge libraries, gives
us some idea of the difficulty of knowing what books were
in these collections, by the comment he makes upon catalogues as they should be:

> They should be scrupulously nice in their Infor-
> mation, taking nothing upon Trust and Hearsay;
> send no Transcripts of ancient Catalogues, instead
> of such as give the present state of their libraries;
> view the books themselves, be sure they are already
> in the Classes referr'd to, and not only in some dis-
> tant and uncertain promise. By these means we
> might truly discover the dormant Riches of the
> nation, and the curious might, with good assurance,
> apply to such Persons as were undoubtedly able to
> answer their Hopes. . . . Till these vast Designs
> are perfected we cannot hope for a full and exact
> Index of all those Historians that have escaped the
> common Destruction in the Dissolution of Abbeys,
> and the Outrages of our Civil Wars.

Another testimony as to the scattered condition of
national records at the end of the eighteenth century is
found in an article by Henry Lemoine, published in the
Gentleman's Magazine Library, 1799. The conditions referred to existed in 1790. Books stored in the Wakefield
Tower were provided with new cases. The White Tower
held records of monasteries, letters of royalty, &c. The
Exchequer books were in the custody of the Lord Treasurer. The Parliament Rolls were in a stone tower in the
old Palace Yard; state papers from the beginning of Henry
VIII to 1790 were stored over a gate going into the cock-
pit. The founding of the British Museum in 1753 was the
first step toward the proper housing of the great collections, and the appointment of the Record Commission in
1800 was the first attempt to systematize and catalogue
the national treasures.

CHRONOLOGICAL TABLE

The following Table exhibits the parallels between the principal Old English publications and interesting events in literary and political history. The italicized parallels refer to American literature.

1566	PARKER: A Testimonie of Antiquitie.	James I of England born.
		UDALL: Ralph Roister Doister (printed).
1568	LAMBARDE: Archainomia.	PARKER: Bishops' Bible. Ascham and Coverdale died.
1570	FOXE: Acts and Monuments (2d ed.).	ASCHAM: Schoolmaster. NORTH: Moral Philosophy of Doni. Sackville and Norton: Gorboduc (2d ed.).
1574	PARKER: Ælfredi Regis Res Gestae.	Mirror for Magistrates, Part 1 (3d ed.). Earl of Leicester's Players licensed.
1576	LAMBARDE: Perambulation of Kent.	GASGOIGNE: Steel Glass. TURBERVILLE: Paradise of Dainty Devices. The Theater and the Curtain built.
1603	CAMDEN: Anglica, Normannica.	FLORIO: Translation of Montaigne's Essays. HEYWOOD: Woman Killed with Kindness (acted). JONSON: Sejanus (acted). SHAKESPEARE: Hamlet (first printed). Accession of James I.
1605	CAMDEN: Remains of a Greater Work. VERSTEGAN: Restitution of Decayed Intelligence.	BACON: Advancement of Learning. JONSON: Volpone (acted). CERVANTES: Don Quixote, Part 1. Dugdale and Sir Thos. Browne born. Gunpowder Plot.

1623 L'ISLE: Saxon Treatise.

BACON: De Augmentis Scientia-
    rum. Historia Vitæ et Mortis.
MASSINGER: Duke of Milan.
SHAKESPEARE: First Folio edition.
WEBSTER: Duchess of Malfi
    (printed).
Camden and Giles Fletcher died.
Pascal born.

1626 H. SPELMAN: Archæologus,
    Part 1.

SANDYS: Translation of Ovid's
    Metamorphoses.
Bacon and Sir John Davies died.
Madame de Sévigné born.

1635 SELDEN: Mare Clausum.

QUARLES: Emblems.
SCUDERY: Ibrahim.
French Academy founded.
Lope de Vega died.

1639 H. SPELMAN: Concilia, De-
    creta, Part 1.

FULLER: History of the Holy War.
CORNEILLE: Horace.
    Cinna.
Wotton died.
Racine born.
First printing-press in America.

1640 J. SPELMAN: Psalterium

CAREW: Poems.
J. HALL: Episcopacy by Divine
    Right.
WALTON: Life of Donne.
WILKINS: Discourse concerning a
    New Planet.
CORNEILLE: Polyeucte.
Burton, Ford, Massinger, Rubens,
    died.
Shadwell and Wycherley born.
Long Parliament meets.
*Bay Psalm Book (first English book
    printed in America).*

1643 WHELOC: Historiæ Ecclesi-
    asticæ Gentis Anglorum
    (Bede and A. S. Chronicle).

BAKER: Chronicle of the Kings of
    England.
BROWNE: Religio Medici.
DAVENANT: Unfortunate Lovers.
MILTON: Doctrine and Discipline
    of Divorce.
PRYNNE: Sovereign Power of Par-
    liaments and Kingdoms

JEREMY TAYLOR: Episcopacy Asserted.

Acta Sanctorum begun by Bollandus.

Accession of Louis XIV.

1644 WHELOC: Archaionomia (Bede, A. S. Chron. and Laws).

MILTON: Areopagitica.

Doctrine and Discipline of Divorce (enlarged).

Tract on Education.

QUARLES: Loyal Convert.

Chillingworth and Quarles died.

Penn born.

Battle of Marsden Moor.

1650 CASAUBON: De Quatuor Linguis.

BAXTER: Saints' Rest.

COWLEY: The Guardian.

FULLER: Pisgah Sight of Palestine.

HOBBES: Human Nature.

De Corpore Politico.

JEREMY TAYLOR: Holy Living.

USSHER: Annales Veteris et Novi Testamenti, Vol. 1.

VAUGHAN: Silex Scintillans.

SCUDERY: Grand Cyrus.

Phineas Fletcher and Descartes died.

1652 TWYSDEN: Historiæ Anglicanæ Scriptores X.

ASHMOLE: Theatrum Chemicum Britannicum.

FILMER: Observations on the Original of Government.

GREVILLE: Life of Sir Philip Sidney.

Milton blind.

Quakers begin to meet as 'Children of Light.'

1655 DUGDALE: Monasticon.

JUNIUS: Cædmon.

MILTON: Defensio contra Morum.

Sonnet on Piedmont Massacres.

PRYNNE: Quakers Unmasked.

STANLEY: History of Philosophy.

JEREMY TAYLOR: Golden Grove.

VAUGHAN: Silex Scintillans, Part 2.

GALILEO: Opere.

13

JOHN COTTON: *A Brief Exposition of Canticles.*

J. COTTON ET AL.: *A Discussion of the Civil Magistrates' Power in Matters of Religion.*

1659 SOMNER: Dictionarium Saxonico-Latino-Anglicum.

CLEVELAND: Poems.

HARRINGTON: Art of Law-giving.

MILTON: Of Civil Power in Ecclesiastical Causes.

RUSHWORTH: Historical   Collections, Vol. 1.

?   : Whole Duty of Man.

MOLIERE: Les Précieuses Ridicules.

JOHN ELIOT: *The Christian Commonwealth.*

1660 SOMNER: Gavelkind.

COWLEY: Ode on the Restoration.

DRYDEN: Astræa Redux.

HARRINGTON: Political Discourses.

MILTON: Easy Way to Establish
a Free Commonwealth.

JEREMY TAYLOR: Ductor Dubitan-
tium.

Worthy Communicant.

USSHER: Chronologia Sacra.

SCUDERY: Almahide.

Pepys begins his diary.

The Restoration of Charles II.

East India Company incorporated.

Royal Society founded.

JOHN ELIOT: *A Tract to Prove that
Indians are Descendants of the
Jews.*

1665 JUNIUS: Quatuor D. N. Jesu
Christi Evangeliorum.

BOYLE: Occasional Reflections.

DRYDEN: Indian Emperor (acted).

MILTON: Paradise   Lost   completed.

WALTON: Life of Hooker.

Controversy between Dryden and
Howard on Dramatic Poetry,
1664-68.

Royal Society: Philosophical Trans-
actions.

The Oxford Gazette founded.

La Rochefoucauld: Maximes.

Journal des Sçavans begun.

1678 WARE: Spelman's Alfredi Magni Vita.

BUNYAN: Pilgrim's Progress, Part 1.

BUTLER: Hudibras, Part 3.

DRYDEN: All for Love.

MARVELL: Growth of Popery and Arbitrary Government.

RYMER: Tragedies of the Last Age considered.

WALTON: Life of Sanderson.

Bolingbroke and Farquhar born.

Marvell died.

JOHN ELIOT: *Harmony of the Gospels.*

1689 HICKES: Institutiones Grammaticæ.

LEE: Princess of Cleve.

LOCKE: Epistola de Tolerantia. Treatise of Civil Government.

SELDEN: Table Talk (printed).

RACINE: Esther.

Montesquieu and Richardson born.

Shadwell, poet laureate.

Accession of William and Mary.

Accession of Peter the Great of Russia.

Toleration Act.

COTTON MATHER: *Memorable Providences relating to Witchcraft.*

1690 USSHER: Historiæ Dogmaticæ (ed. Wharton).

DRYDEN: Amphitryon.

LOCKE: Essay concerning Human Understanding. Second Treatise of Civil Government.

JAMES ALLEN ET AL.: *Principles of Protestant Religion Maintained.*

1691 WHARTON: Anglia Sacra.

LOCKE: Considerations on the Lowering of Interest.

NORRIS: Ideal World.

NORTH: Discourse of Trade.

PETTY: Political Anatomy of Ireland.

RAY: Wisdom of God manifested in Creation.

WOOD: Athenæ Oxonienses, Vol. 1.

RACINE: Athalie.

Baxter died.

COTTON MATHER: *Triumphs of the Reformed Religion in America.*

1692 GIBSON: Chronicon Saxonicum.

DENNIS: Impartial Critic.
DRYDEN: Eleonora.
LOCKE: Third Letter for Tolera-
tion.
TEMPLE: Essays.
Lee and Shadwell died.
Tate poet laureate.
INCREASE MATHER: *Further Ac-
count of New England Witches.*

1698 THWAITES: Heptateuchus.
RAWLINSON: Boethius.

COLLIER: Short View of the Im-
morality of the Stage.
CROWNE: Caligula.
ALGERNON SIDNEY: Discourse on
Government.
VANBRUGH: Provoked Wife.
Howard died.
Warburton born.
Peter the Great visited England.
COTTON MATHER: *Eleutheria, or an
Idea of the Reformation in Eng-
land.*

1701 BENSON: Vocabularium An-
glo-Saxonicum (Somner's
Dictionary, condensed).
ELSTOB: Sermo Lupi.

DEFOE: True-born Englishman.
DENNIS: Advancement of Modern
Poetry.
FARQUHAR: Sir Harry Wildair.
STEELE: Christian Hero.
SWIFT: Contest between the Nobles
and Commons in Athens and
Rome.
Accession of Frederick I of Prussia.
War of Spanish Succession.

{ 1703 HICKES: Thesaurus.
{ 1705 WANLEY: Catalogus.

FARQUHAR: The Inconstant.

ROWE: Fair Penitent.
STEELE: Lying Lover.
Pepys died.
John Wesley born.
ADDISON: The Campaign.
CIBBER: Careless Husband.
CLARENDON: History of the Great
Rebellion (pub. 1704-07).
DEFOE: The Review.
R. NELSON: Festivals and Fasts of
the Christian Church.
NEWTON: Optics.
RYMER: Foedera, Vol. 1.

SWIFT: Battle of the Books.
Tale of a Tub.
WYCHERLEY: Poems.
Locke died.
Alfieri born.
Battle of Blenheim.
ADDISON: Remarks on Several
Parts of Italy.
STEELE: Tender Husband.
VANBRUGH: The Confederacy.
ROBERT BEVERLEY: *History of Virginia (pub. in London).*

1708 WOTTON: Conspectus of
Hickes' Thesaurus.

COLLIER: Ecclesiastical History of
Great Britain, Vol. 1.
MOTTEUX AND URQUHART: Translation of Rabelais.
OCKLEY: History of the Saracens,
Vol. 1.
PHILIPS: Cyder.
SWIFT: Argument against abolishing Christianity.
Predictions of Isaac Bickerstaff.
William Pitt born.

1709 E. ELSTOB: An English-
Saxon Homily.

BERKELEY: New Theory of Vision.
DEFOE: History of the Union.
AMBROSE PHILIPS: Pastorals.
POPE: Pastorals.
PRIOR: Poems.
ROWE: Edition of Shakespeare.
STEELE AND ADDISON: The Tatler.
STRYPE: Annals of the Reformation, Vol. 1.
SWIFT: Project for the Advancement of Christianity.
Vindication of Isaac Bickerstaff.
Johnson born.
EXPERIENCE MAYHEW: *Psalms and St. John's Gospel in Indian and English.*

1711 THWAITES: Grammatica.

ATTERBURY: State of Religion.
DENNIS: Reflections on an Essay
upon Criticism.
POPE: Essay on Criticism.
SHAFTSBURY: Characteristics.

STEELE AND ADDISON: The Spectator.

STRYPE: Life of Parker.

SWIFT: Windsor Prophesy.
Miscellanies.

Boileau died.

Hume born.

Accession of Charles VI.

1715 E. ELSTOB: Rudiments of Grammar for the English-Saxon Tongue.
English-Saxon Homilies of Ælfric (not published).

ADDISON: The Freeholder.

DEFOE: Appeal to Honour and Justice.

GAY: Trivia.
The Fan.

POPE: Temple of Fame.
Translation of Iliad, Bks. 1-4.

ROWE: Lade Jane Grey.

TICKELL: Translation of Iliad, Bk. 1.

LE SAGE: Gil Blas, Bks. 1-3.

Burnet, Fenelon, R. Nelson, Tate, Wycherley died.

Rowe, poet laureate.

Jacobite Rebellion.

Accession of Louis XV.

LAWRENCE CLAESSE: *Morning and Evening Prayer, etc., translated into Mohawk Indian language.*

1720 HEARNE: Textus Roffensis.

DEFOE: Robinson Crusoe, Parts 2 and 3.
Captain Singleton.
Memories of a Cavalier.

NEAL: History of New England.

POPE: Translation of Iliad completed.

WATTS: Divine and Moral Songs.

South Sea Bubble.

1721 WILKINS: Leges Anglo-Saxonicæ.

ADDISON: Dialogues upon Medals.
Evidences of the Christian Religion.

BAILEY: Universal English Dictionary.

RAMSAY: Poems.

STRYPE: Ecclesiastical Memorials, Vol. 1.

MONTESQUIEU: Lettres Persaues.

Watteau died.

Walpole prime minister.

JEREMIAH DRUMOR: *Defense of New England Charters.*

COTTON MATHER: *Christian Philosopher.*

1722 SMITH: Alfred's Bede.
WISE: Annales Rerum Gestarum Ælfredi Magni.

DEFOE: Colonel Jack.
Moll Flanders.
Journal of the Plague Year.
PARNELL: Poems.
STEELE: Conscious Lovers.
DANIEL COXE: *A Description of La Louisiana, &c.*

1735 WOTTON: Conspectus of Hickes' Thesaurus.

BOLINGBROKE: Dissertation on Parties.
JOHNSON: Translation of Loba's Voyage to Abyssinia.
LYTTLETON: Letters from a Persian in England.
POPE: Epistle to Dr. Arbuthnot. Correspondence.
SOMERVILLE: The Chase.
LE SAGE: Gil Blas, Bks. 7-12.
LINNAEUS: Systema Naturæ.
Arbuthnot died.
Voyage of the Wesleys to America.
JUDAH MONIS: *Grammar of the Hebrew Tongue.*

1737 WILKINS: Concilia.

CRUDEN: Concordance to the Scriptures.
FIELDING: The Historical Register.
GREEN: The Spleen.
LILLO: Fatal Curiosity.
POPE: Imitations from Horace.
SHENSTONE: Poems. Schoolmistress.
WHISTON: Translation of Josephus' History of the Jews.
Strype died.
Gibbon born.
Prince of Wales opposes the Walpole ministry.

1743 LYE: Junius' Etymologicum

BENTLEY: Remarks on a Late Discourse on Freethinking.
BLAIR: The Grave.
FIELDING: Jonathan Wild.

SHENSTONE: Pastoral Ballad.
American Philosophical Society founded.
First Bible printed in America in a European Language (Cambridge).
THOMAS CLAP: *Introduction to the Study of Philosophy.*
G. FOX: *Instruction for Right Spelling, &c.*

1772 MANNING: Dictionarium Saxonico-Latinum.

CUMBERLAND: Fashionable Lover.
FOOTE: The Nabob.
JUNIUS: Letters (collected edition).
LESSING: Emilia Galotti.
Coleridge and Schlegel born.

1773 BARRINGTON: Alfred's Orosius.

BARBAULD: Poems.
HESTER CHAPONE: Letters on the Improvement of the Mind.
GOLDSMITH: She Stoops to Conquer.
HAWKESWORTH: Voyages.
SMOLLETT: Ode to Independence.
BÜRGER: Lenore.
GOETHE: Gotz von Berlichingen.
Chesterfield died.
Sismondi born.

1788 MANNING: King Alfred's Will.

GIBBON: Decline and Fall of the Roman Empire.
HESTER THRALE: Letters from Dr. Johnson.
KANT: Kritik der Praktischen Vernunft.
ST. PIERRE: Paul et Virginie.
'The Times' founded.
Buffon died.
Byron born.

BIBLIOGRAPHY

This bibliography aims to present references of two kinds: (a) books which give the fullest information approximately contemporary with recorded events; (b) books which have furnished the best clues to materials. The best sources of information are to be found in the prefaces of the books discussed in the thesis. These and other specific references are indicated in footnotes.

EDWARDS, EDWARD. Memoirs of Libraries. New edition, London, 1901.

ELLIS, HENRY. Letters of Eminent Literary Men. London, 1843.

HALLIWELL, J. O. Autobiography of Sir Simonds D'Ewes. London, 1845.

MICHEL, FRANCISQUE. Bibliothèque Anglo-Saxonne. Paris, 1837.

MORES, EDWARD ROWE. Dissertation on English Typographical Founders. London, 1778.

NICHOLS, JOHN. Bishop Nicolson's Correspondence. London, 1809.

————— —————. Literary Anecdotes. London, 1812.

NICOLSON, WILLIAM. English Historical Library. London, 1696.

PAUL, HERMANN. Grundriss der Germanischen Philologie. Strassburg, 1889.

PETHERAM, JOHN. The Progress and Present State of Anglo-Saxon Literature. London, 1840.

PLOMER, H. R. Dictionary of Book-Sellers and Printers. London, 1907.

STRYPE, JOHN. Life and Acts of Matthew Parker. London, 1711.

WANLEY, HUMPHREY. Catalogus Historico-Criticus. Oxford, 1705.

WOOD, ANTHONY À. Athenæ Oxonienses. London, 1813.

WÜLKER, RICHARD. Grundriss zur Geschichte der Angelsächsischen Litteratur. Leipzig, 1885.

INDEX

A

Ælfredi Regis Res Gestæ cf. Parker, Matthew.

Anglo-Saxon types, 157 f.; first used in Oxford, 64, 165; Junian, 165 f.; Fell, 167; Elstob, 168 f.; Star Chamber founders of, 172; Chart of printers using, 173 f.

Archæologus, cf. Spelman, Sir Henry.

Archaionomia, cf. Lambarde, William.

Asser's *Ælfredi Regis Res Gestæ,* Parker's edition, 33 f.

B

Badger, Richard, O. E. printer, 163.

Bale, John, 13 f., preface to Leland's *Laboryouse Journey,* 182.

Barringtcn, Daines, edits *Orosius,* 106.

Bishop, William, letter of, 137.

Boswell, Sir William, letter of, 115.

C

Camdem, William, interest in O. E. antiquities, 43.

Cave, William, 82.

Charlett, Arthur, patron of O. E. scholarship, 102.

Concilia, cf. Spelman, Sir Henry.

Cotton, Sir John, letter of, 118.

Cotton, Sir Robert, library of, 187 f.

D

Daniel, Roger, O. E. printer, 163.

Day, John, O. E. printer, 23, 27, 158, 170.

De Antiquitate Britannicæ Ecclesiæ, cf. Parker, Matthew.

Defence of Priestes' Marriages, 26.

Dictionaries of 'Saxon' attempted, 56, 105.

Dugdale, Sir William, edits Spelman's *Archæologus,* 49; the *Monasticon* of, 69; letter of, 118.

E

Elstob, Elizabeth, *Rudiment of Grammar,* 91; biography, 93 f.; *Homilies,* 95; preface to the *Homily on the Birthday of St. Gregory,* 145 f.; preface to the *Rudiments of Grammar.* 148 ff.; letters of, 133, 134.

Elstob, William, O. E. scholar, 93 f.

Etymologicum, cf. Junius and Lye.

F

Fell, John, patron of O. E. scholarship, 73.

Flesher, Miles, O. E. printer, 163.

Flacius, Matthias, influence on Parker, 14.

Foxe, John *Book of Martyrs,* 31; editon of the Gospels in O. E., 31; relation to the 'Bishops Bible', 32.

G

Gazophylacium Anglicanum, 82.

Gibson, Edmund, 76; letters of, 119, 131, 138.

Guide into Tongues, cf. Minsheu, John.

H

Hakluyt, Richard, translations from *Orosius,* 37.

Haviland, John, O. E. printer, 160.

Hearne, Thomas, edits *Textus Roffensis,* 96; antiquarian interest in O. E., 97 f.

Heptateuchus, cf. Thwaites, Edward.

Hickes, George, criticism of Lambarde's *Archaionomia,* 29; 75; O. E. grammars of, 86 f.; *Thesaurus* of 88 f.; 91, 103; controversial works, 93; letters of, 128, 132-136.

Hodgkinsonne, Richard, O. E. printer, 162.

Holinshed, Raphael, prints charter of William, 37.

Homily on the Birthday of St. Gregory cf. Elstob, Elizabeth.

Hudson, John, 103.